Sasha Fenton's
Reading the Future

Sasha Fenton's
Reading the Future

Your Step-by-Step Guide

to Predictive Astrology

ZAMBEZI PUBLISHING LTD

Published in 2012 by
Zambezi Publishing Ltd
P.O. Box 221, Plymouth
Devon PL2 2YJ
www.zampub.com   info@zampub.com

Originally published in the UK in 1996
by Judy Piatkus (Publishers) Ltd
Updated & revised edition published in the UK in 2012
by Zambezi Publishing Ltd

Copyright © 1995-2012 Sasha Fenton
Sasha Fenton asserts the moral right
to be identified as the author of this work
in terms of the Copyright, Designs and Patents Act 1988
British Library Cataloguing in Publication Data:
A catalogue record for this book
is available from the British Library

Illustrations © 2012 Jan Budkowski
Cover © 2012 Jan Budkowski
Edited by Jan Budkowski
Typeset by Zambezi Publishing Ltd, Plymouth UK
Printed and bound in the UK by Lightning Source (UK) Ltd
Digitally published by Zambezi Publishing Ltd

Printed edition ISBN 978-1-903065-77-8

All rights reserved. No part of this publication may be reproduced, stored in a retrieval system, or transmitted in any form or by any means, electronic, mechanical, photocopying, recording or otherwise, without the prior written permission of the publisher. This book is sold subject to the condition that it shall not, by way of trade or otherwise, be lent, resold, hired out or otherwise circulated without the publisher's prior written consent, in any form of binding, cover or format other than that in which it is originally published, and without a similar condition being imposed on the subsequent purchaser. No warranties, either express or implied, are made by the author or the publisher regarding the contents of this book. The intention is to provide general information regarding the subject matter, and neither the author or the publisher shall have any responsibility to any person or entity in respect of any loss or damage caused or alleged to be caused, directly or indirectly, by the use or misuse of information contained in this book. If expert guidance is required, the services of a professional consultant should be sought. By reading this book, you agree to be bound by the above.

About the Author

Sasha became a professional consultant astrologer in 1973, but had to tail off her consultancy business once her writing took off. She has written over 126 books, mainly on mind, body and spirit subjects, with sales of around 6.5 million copies to her credit, and translations of some titles into a dozen languages. Sasha wrote the stars columns for several British newspapers and magazines, and contributed a chapter to "Llewellyn's Sun Sign Book" every year for ten years. She is currently the Chinese Astrology columnist for Prediction Magazine.

Having broadcast regularly all over the UK and in several other countries at times, she has also lectured widely, including festivals in various parts of the UK and Sydney, Melbourne, Johannesburg and Cape Town.

Sasha has been President of the British Astrological and Psychic Society (BAPS), Chair and Treasurer for the British Advisory Panel on Astrological Education (APAE), and a member of the Executive Council of the Writers' Guild of Great Britain.

Sasha's first husband, Tony Fenton, died of cancer and diabetes related problems. She met her second husband, Jan Budkowski, in South Africa and their first home was a tent on the banks of the Zambezi River in Jan's country of birth, Zambia. They married and settled in the west of England, where they now run Zambezi Publishing Ltd. Sasha has two children, three grandchildren and a dog named Pippa.

Dedication

For Jonathan Dee, now sadly passed away,
who was my constant source of inspiration and comfort.

Contents

Introduction	*1*
Chapter One: **For Beginners**	*3*
Chapter Two: **Transits**	*9*
Chapter Three: **Progressions**	*11*
Chapter Four: **Other Techniques**	*15*
Chapter Five: **Hand Calculations for Progressions**	*19*
Chapter Six: **Further Methods, Ideas and Information**	*23*
Chapter Seven: **The Interpretation Maze**	*27*
Chapter Eight: **Progression & Transit Aspects**	*35*
Chapter Nine: **Solar Arcs & Returns**	*45*
Chapter Ten: **Moon Phases & Eclipses**	*47*
Chapter Eleven: **The Cycles of Time**	*49*
Chapter Twelve: **Recap: The Right Method for Each Job**	*57*
Chapter Thirteen: **Astrology and the Body**	*59*
Chapter Fourteen: **Signs of the Zodiac**	*63*

Chapter Fifteen:
The Sun through the Signs & Houses — 69

Chapter Sixteen:
The Moon through the Signs and Houses — 77

Chapter Seventeen:
Solar Aspects — 85

Chapter Eighteen:
Lunar Aspects — 93

Chapter Nineteen:
Planetary Aspects — 101

Chapter Twenty:
The Slower Moving Planets — 113

Conclusion — 119

Index — 121

Introduction

In this book, I show you how to use astrology to predict the future, starting with some very simple methods suitable for a complete beginner. Later, I focus on the most popular and most useful techniques, and then look into some that are used less frequently. There is nothing magical about the astrological concept of "reading the future"... if you know the effect that a planetary aspect or configuration has, and you know from the planets' regular orbits when a particular aspect is going to happen, you can foretell what effect is likely to take place at that time. Pretty much the same ideas as any doctor telling a pregnant woman what exactly is going to happen, and when, as far as her pregnancy is concerned.

When I wrote the original version of this book way back in the mid-1990s, I had already been using astrology software for over a decade, but that was still fairly unusual in those days. Now, most people have access to a computer, and even the most complex professional astrology software is much less expensive than it was, while there is always something cheap but useful to be found on Amazon or eBay for under £50, and sometimes even for less than £10. Even the cheapest program should produce an excellent natal chart, along with a lengthy interpretation printout. Some also give planetary transits for the coming year, along with full interpretations, while others offer compatibility charts that show how people can expect to get along together.

For those who want to learn more, a browse through the various astrology magazines will introduce you to schools, courses and quality software houses. Course fees are usually spread over the duration of the course, and you can buy software on a credit card and pay it off over a few months, so it is easier than ever these days for someone to learn astrology. A friend of mine recently completed the course run by the British Astrological and Psychic Society (BAPS), and she is now working as a professional astrologer.

Astrology schools no longer bother to teach hand calculating, and rely on computerisation, but in this book, I still show the hand calculation methods for day-for-a-year progressions, because you might want to look into this right away, without waiting until you have appropriate software.

Whatever level you are at, you will need to buy some astrology tables. You can now buy an ephemeris (book of tables) to cover the whole of the 20th century and the first fifty years of the 21st century. In addition to these, you will need the little "Raphael's Ephemeris" for the current year. For instance, I am writing this during 2011, so my well thumbed, current "Raphael's" is for 2011, but before this book has been published, I will no doubt have bought the "Raphael's" for 2012 as well. I love the little Raphael's books, as they give an instant picture of all that is going on, and they are easy to carry around.

If you enjoy reading astrology books, buy lots of different ones, because different writers will give you information on various areas of astrology.

At the end of this book, I list very brief interpretations that you can use for any transit and progression, and these will act as prompts, or stir your own insight and intuition, and they will give you something to get your teeth into until you can buy more books and read more about the subject. Having said all the above, there's no doubt that you will learn the most by doing charts for people and by getting their feedback.

I hope you enjoy this updated and improved version of my earlier book. I certainly enjoyed writing it - both times!

Chapter One:
For Beginners

If you need to check out your own Sun sign, look at the following list. The Sun doesn't change sign on exactly the same day each year, so if your birthday is "on the cusp", you will have to look up the Sun's position for your date and time of birth in an ephemeris. I've even come across twins with different Sun signs, because the Sun changed sign just after one twin was born.

Aries	March 21 to April 20
Taurus	April 21 to May 21
Gemini	May 22 to June 21
Cancer	June 22 to July 23
Leo	July 24 to August 23
Virgo	August 24 to September 23
Libra	September 24 to October 23
Scorpio	October 24 to November 22
Sagittarius	November 23 to December 21
Capricorn	December 22 to January 20
Aquarius	January 21 to February 19
Pisces	February 20 to March 20

People often ask if being born close to another sign means that their characters are influenced by the adjacent sign. Some astrologers think that this is so, while others are equally adamant that this is not the case. My feeling is that the person born at the end of a sign will be influenced by the next sign along, as it is coming towards them, so to speak.

Timing of Events

There are certain times of the year when things go well for all of us, and other times when they can be almost guaranteed to go wrong. Some people always have a terrible Christmas, while others dread some other time of the year. The calendars pictured in this chapter will help you to find those months that are likely to be harmonious or difficult for you.

Generally speaking, most people have mixed feelings about life around the time of their birthdays. We all enjoy receiving cards and presents, but we hate getting older. These mixed feelings are typical of a planetary conjunction, which is where a planet's current position in the sky is crossing the position of any of those on our own natal horoscopes. At the time of your birthday, a number of planets will be passing close to those that are on your birth chart, so the mixed feelings are to be expected.

If you write the months of the year down on a piece of paper in a circular or "clock" form, you will be able to find the month opposite to your own birth month. This will be six months after your own birth month. This is likely to be a "down" time, when you will feel ill or out of sorts. You may be "up to your neck in things" when the Sun is square to your own birth month - these times being three or nine months after your own birth month. On the other hand, you should feel in command of yourself and your life when the Sun is two, four, eight or ten months away from your birthday.

The following example shows you how to use the system. The first list is for someone born in May, while you should use the second one for your own birthday, whenever that happens to be. If you wish, you can copy these lists and experiment with them.

CALENDAR LIST	
AN EXAMPLE FOR SOMEONE BORN IN MAY	
May	Important
June	Pleasant
July	Excellent
August	Difficult
September	Excellent
October	Awkward
November	Challenging
December	Troublesome
January	Excellent
February	Difficult
March	Excellent
April	Depressing

1: For Beginners

For Any Birth Month

*List your birth month first,
and the succeeding months in order*

Your Own Calendar List	
Birth Month:	
	Important
	Pleasant
	Excellent
	Difficult
	Excellent
	Awkward
	Challenging
	Troublesome
	Excellent
	Difficult
	Excellent
	Depressing

The Astrologer's Calendar

Just as the months on a calendar always begin with January and end in December, so the zodiac signs always start with Aries and end with Pisces. Start with your own sign and then list the others in the following order.

Aries
Taurus
Gemini
Cancer
Leo
Virgo
Libra
Scorpio
Sagittarius
Capricorn
Aquarius
Pisces

The following Zodiac List will demonstrate the times of the year when you are feeling good or downhearted, and the only difference between this and the Calendar List is the terminology.

The Zodiac List

Put your own sign of the zodiac first, then the next, then the one after that, etc.

ZODIAC SIGN:	
	Important
	Pleasant
	Excellent
	Difficult
	Excellent
	Awkward
	Challenging
	Troublesome
	Excellent
	Difficult
	Excellent
	Depressing

Now, if you express this list as a clock-shaped circle, with your birth month on the left hand side in the nine o'clock position, you will begin to think like an astrologer. Here is an example that starts with Virgo:

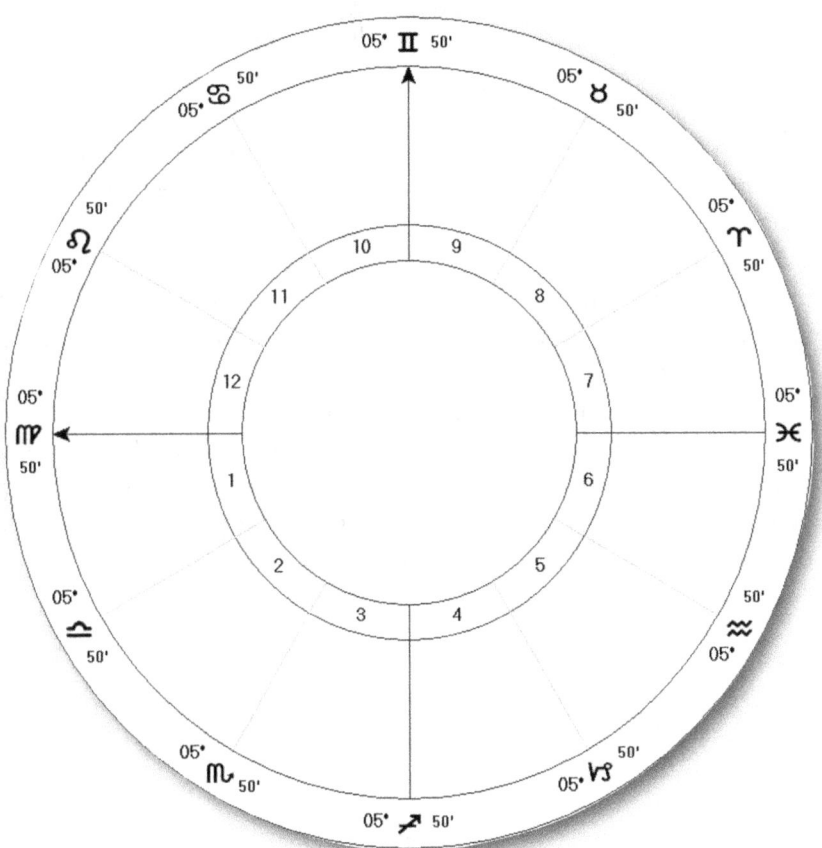

What Comes Next?

Up to now, we've been looking at techniques that don't require any astrological know-how, but from this point onwards, you really do need to be able to put together and understand a birthchart. You can learn natal charting from books, correspondence courses, and evening classes or from an astrologer who is willing to show you the basics for a fee. A search of the 'Net will probably throw up lots of courses.

A natal or birth chart is a picture of the planets' positions in the sky at the moment of a person's birth at the place of their birth. The starting point of any natal chart is the ascendant. This is the point directly to the left of the chart, where nine o'clock would be on a clock face. The ascendant offers information on the childhood and background of the subject and also of the early programming that went on in his life. The twelve astrological houses are marked around in an anti-clockwise direction from the ascendant. These houses can be of equal size or unequal size, depending upon which house system is used. There are many house systems in use, but if you are just getting into astrology, I suggest that you use the equal house method. Later you may decide that you prefer the popular Placidus method or some less popular method, such as Koch.

The Signs that the Sun, Moon and planets occupy all show how these heavenly bodies influence us, while the Houses show how these planets are put to use. If you think in terms of an implement, the sign could represent a food mixer, a cricket bat, a broom or a gun, but the house shows the purpose that you put these things to.

For instance, a subject with Mercury (the planet that rules his ability to think) in Aquarius would have an analytical mind that is attuned to new ideas and new technology. If it were in the sixth house, he would use this for his work or to solve health problems.

Chapter Two:
Transits

On a clear night, take a look at the sky and remind yourself that the planets don't only live in the pages of your ephemeris or in the workings of your computer. They are real and they are in the heavens, working their magic on us at every twist and turn of their orbits. Just before dawn on a cloudless morning, you will notice two or three stars that seem to hang about after the others have gone. Alternatively, wait for a cloudless night just after the Sun has set, and you will notice two or three stars shining brightly in the dark blue heavens. These "stars" are actually planets, they don't twinkle like real stars, and the chances are that if you look towards the area where the Sun is rising or setting, you will spot bright and beautiful Venus and the smaller and duller, Mercury. Elsewhere in the sky, depending upon the time of year, you may find another very bright planet, which is Jupiter, and perhaps the smaller and slightly reddish Mars, or the similarly small but slightly yellowish Saturn. You will need an astronomer's telescope to see Uranus or Neptune, or the dwarf planet, Pluto and the planetoid, Chiron.

Depending upon whether you have cheapo software or more sophisticated astrology software, you should generate your natal chart and a separate transit chart for today, or generate your natal chart and ask your software to show the transit chart around it. Alternatively, you can use the ephemeris to check out today's planets positions against your natal chart.

Interpreting the Transits

Planets move at different speeds. A lunar transit will be over within hours, while Pluto's effect will be around for a couple of years at least. If your ephemeris suggests that there will be an eclipse or an interesting conjunction in the sky, and if the night happens to be a clear one, go outside and look, because I guarantee that you will feel a rush of excitement by seeing your ephemeris come to life in the sky.

An Example of Transits

This chart belongs to my friend, the late Jonathan Dee, who suffered bereavement on 2 June 1993, and I have Jonathan's permission to write about this unhappy event. Jon's partner had probably been ill with stomach trouble for some time, but had not been aware of the potential gravity of the situation. A road accident in April meant a short spell in hospital and it was the shock of this that brought the underlying problem to the surface. Over the next few weeks, Jon's partner became progressively more ill, and then he died.

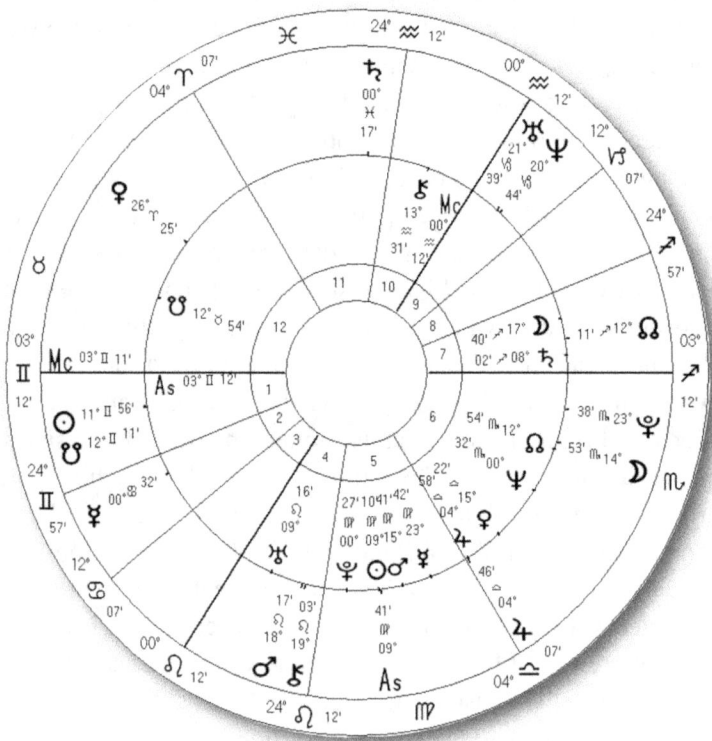

Jonathan's chart showed transiting Saturn slowing down before turning retrograde at zero degrees of Pisces, opposing Jonathan's natal Pluto at zero degrees of Virgo. Transiting Jupiter was conjunct natal Jupiter (Jupiter return), and also moving from retrograde to direct motion. Transiting Mars would soon also cross Pluto, also at zero degrees of Virgo, and Venus was about to cross the south node.

A retrograde transit is never easy to live with, and Saturn, Pluto and Mars can all be considered as "malefic" planets. Jupiter can be a happy-go-lucky planet, but it can also be difficult, especially if other features on the chart are causing difficulties. Venus can indicate partnership matters and the nodes can indicate a karmic or unavoidably fated event.

Chapter Three: Progressions

Let's start by demystifying some of the amazing terminology used to describe the various forms of chart manipulation. Sometimes there are several names for the same method. The following list covers most of the terms that you are likely to come across, and you will soon see that this isn't as daunting as it looks.

The only forms of predictive astrology that I will cover in detail are day-for-a-year progressions (also known as secondary directions), solar returns, lunar returns and solar arc progressions.

1. Progressions
2. Day-for-a-year progressions
3. Secondary directions
4. Secondary progressions
5. Primary directions
6. Solar arc directions
7. Solar arc progressions
8. Solar arc MC progressions
9. One-degree progressions
10. Tertiary progressions
11. Minor progressions
12. Daily house progressions
13. Duodenary progressions
14. Converse directions
15. Converse progressions

Progressions

This name simply covers any method of progressing a horoscope, therefore anything that moves a chart by some form of mathematical calculation. If an astrologer talks about progressions or a progressed horoscope, the chances are that he is talking about the most popular method of them all, that is, the day-for-a-year (secondary direction) method.

Converse Progressions

This means progressing the chart backwards! Many modern computer programs will happily provide converse progressions, so enthusiastic student astrologers should have a go at one or two of these in order to satisfy their curiosity. They can sometimes reveal interesting events.

Day-for-a-year Progressions, Secondary Progressions, Secondary Directions

All these terms mean exactly the same thing! Most astrologers just say "progressions", but for the purposes of this book, I am using the term, "day-for-a-year progressions". These are not difficult to do by hand and they are available on every astrological computer program.

Unfortunately, computer programs are usually American in origin, and American astrologers tend to make up their own names for everything! The Solar Fire program calls this method "Solar Arc MC progressions". This is not clever, because this can be confused with the Solar Arc method, which is not the same.

Solar Arc Directions, Primary Directions, One-Degree Progressions, Solar Arc Directed Charts

Most professional astrologers call these "solar arc progressions" or "solar arc directions".

This is very easy do by hand, and instantaneous when done by a computer. All you do is take each planet and move it one degree for each year of life. Technically speaking, there is a slight difference between the different terms, because the one-degree progressions simply move everything forward by one degree, while the other methods may move the chart forward by the same amount in each year as the daily motion of either the midheaven or the Sun. As both of these move at a touch less than one degree per year, the results are much the same. If you need to be really accurate, use a computer.

As an astrologer, I find the solar arc technique a bit crude, because it doesn't take account of the difference in speed that each of the planets moves, and it ignores the possibility of retrograde motion. However, it is worth progressing the Sun and the midheaven by this method, and taking a look at what shows up.

Progressing the midheaven one degree per year can be a very handy tool when trying to rectify a chart, in order to work out exactly when someone was born. I'll describe this technique for you at the end of this chapter, because it's useful.

Tertiary Progressions

This moves the chart by one day for a Lunar month (27.32 days). You can't do this properly without a computer. This one is fun to play about with, but not worth using seriously.

Minor Progressions

This method substitutes a Lunar month (27.32 days) for a year. This is also interesting, but you can't even think about doing it properly without a computer. Like the tertiary progressions, this one is not worth spending too much time or energy on.

Duodenary Progressions

Divide each sign by twelve divisions of two-and-a-half degrees each. Progress each planet and angle by one two-and-a-half degree segment for each year of life. This relates to the Dwaads used in Hindu astrology, which I have written about in "The Hidden Zodiac".

Chapter Four:
Other Techniques

Continuing from the list in the previous chapter, here are the rest of the techniques we need to mention:

16 90-degree arc
17 Solar returns
18 Solar return directions
19 Lunar returns
20 Venusian arcs
21 Martial arcs
22 Decumbitures
23 Horary astrology
24 Electional astrology
25 Mundane astrology
26 The perpetual noon date method!

90-Degree Arc

This is a very different form of astrology, and while it does have its adherents, those who use this method don't use our own familiar forms of astrology at all. I have looked into it, and I can understand and use it, but I can't see any value in dumping our familiar forms of astrology for this method. The method breaks the chart down into its component elements of fire, earth, air and water, and then puts all the fire segments together in one area. The method even progresses each of the element "blocks" in turn. Decent astro-software may be able to produce these charts for you.

Solar Returns, Solar Return Directions

I consider this method to be a handy tool, and it can sometimes be more informative than the day-for-a-year method.

This is very tricky to work out by hand, but very easy on a computer. The idea is to place the Sun in the exact degree and minute that it occupied at the moment of birth. This is actually a transit chart for the anniversary of the moment of birth in any year. When glanced at quickly, Solar returns seem to offer a flavour of what the year ahead will bring, and the ascendant in particular gives a strong picture of what the coming year will feel like. However, when looked at methodically, a solar return chart can be very revealing.

Tip:
You'll usually get the best results by putting your progressed or transit chart around a natal chart and seeing how the new planetary positions affect the original ones, but solar and lunar return charts work best when looked at in their own right, without being placed against any other kind of chart.

Lunar Returns

The idea is to place the Moon at the exact degree and minute that it occupied in the natal chart, and then array the rest of the chart around this new position, with the ascendant and midheaven, etc. all carefully recalculated. This offers a flavour of the month in question. When looking at a lunar return, the mood and even the events that show up may come into being a bit before the lunar return, or they may only come into being as it comes to an end. This is a job for a computer.

Venusian Arcs and Martian arcs

The idea here is similar to solar arc directions. That is, to move the whole chart by the amount that either Venus or Mars would have travelled during the course of a number of years. As both of these planets appear to move at varying speeds and also change from forward motion into retrograde motion and back again from time to time, this is obviously one for an Einstein to play with. I don't even know of a computer program that can tackle these. Forget them!

Decumbitures

This is a fascinating area of astrology, and it is used to diagnose and plot the history of an illness. It's associated with the ancient medical ideas of the "humours". In the olden days, the herbalist, Nicholas Culpeper and the astrologer, William Lilly used Decumbitures. A few specialists in astrology and herbal medicines still use this method, one of the most noteworthy modern proponents being Dylan Warren-Davis.

4: OTHER TECHNIQUES

Decumbitures follow ancient and specialised rules, and are beyond the scope of this book.

Using Horary Astrology to Answer Questions

This is an ancient method of prediction that has recently come back into favour. It is based on the idea that one makes up a chart for the moment that a question is asked, and then the chart is assessed in order to find the answer. This can be done by following normal astrological systems, but true horary astrology has many rules of its own. This takes a lot of study before one can become competent.

A Simple Semi-Horary Method

Set up a chart for the time that you first set out on a course of action or for the moment when you ask a particular question, and then interpret the chart as you would a person or a situation. Use the usual rules for natal charting, but add a touch of intuition to your reading. Don't forget to use House Rulers. For example, I recently set up to do something creative with a partner, and both the seventh and eighth house (on a Placidus chart system) were ruled by Pisces. This would not be a great idea for a normal business venture, but quite good for a creative one. This was especially so as Neptune (the ruler of the seventh and eighth) was well aspected in the fifth house.

Electional Astrology

The idea is to pick the right moment for something that you want to do. This is typically used in India and throughout the east, in order to select the best day and time for a marriage or for the start of an important enterprise. What the astrologer is trying to do here is to give the marriage or enterprise the best possible chance of success, not just on the day it starts, but over time. Many astrologers use this method for choosing the right time to do something important.

Mundane Astrology

The term mundane here means "of the world" and it refers to the fortunes of cities, countries, political parties or any other kind of organisation. Mundane astrology means that one makes up a natal chart to show the character of the organisation, town or country in question. All the usual predictive techniques can be used against this natal chart. If you want to work for any form of the media, this is an important form of astrology. If you have even the slightest intention of looking into this method, you will need to get two books written by Nick Campion. The first is called "Mundane Astrology" and the second is "The Book of World Horoscopes".

Daily House Progressions

I found this on my latest computer program, but just what it is isn't clear! The program manual doesn't give much of a clue either. The planets appear to be progressed by the usual day-for-a-year method, but the ascendant and houses are different.

Perpetual Noon Date

This is an old-fashioned method that is difficult and long-winded. It's not worth bothering with.

Rectification with the Midheaven

Here is a useful aid to working out the exact time of a person's birth, but it will only work if the subject has at least some idea of when he was born. Take the earliest and the latest times at which the subject thinks he may have been born, and make up a chart for the middle of these. Then ask the "client" to pick an incident out of his childhood for you to use as a "hook" to hang the chart on. An obvious one would be the date that he started school, particularly if this was traumatic. Other ideas would be of a childhood accident, a move of house or anything else that stands out in your subject's mind. Now, move the midheaven forward by a degree for a year and see if it makes any aspect to any appropriate planet, or any other hot spot (such as an angle) at the age in question. If it does, then take another incident and try again. If you get the timing on at least two events right, you have very likely found the correct time of birth. If the events seem to come about a little before or after the midheaven transit, then your birth time is out one way or the other and can then be easily adjusted.

An appropriate planet for a child having an accident could be Mars, or the planet that rules the part of the body that was hurt, so a broken hip would be a Jupiter matter. A move of house or a family problem would involve the Moon, while happiness or unhappiness at school would suggest a Mercury situation. An ailment would connect with whatever planet ruled the part of the body that was sick, such as Jupiter for jaundice or Venus for tonsillitis. Watch for the signs and houses in which events occur.

Chapter Five:
Hand Calculations for Progressions

While you're waiting to buy more sophisticated astrology software, you can do your day-for-a-year progressions by hand. This method is rough and ready, but it works well enough. The example that I use here is for a mythical person called Fred who was born in London, England at 10pm on the 1st of July 1980. Before you do any progressions, you need an Ephemeris and a printout of the natal chart to work with, so here is Fred's chart. I haven't given a specific date for Fred's progressed chart (shown further on), just simply shown the method, so you can use the method to look at his situation during any year of his life, from infancy to the current year, or for any future year.

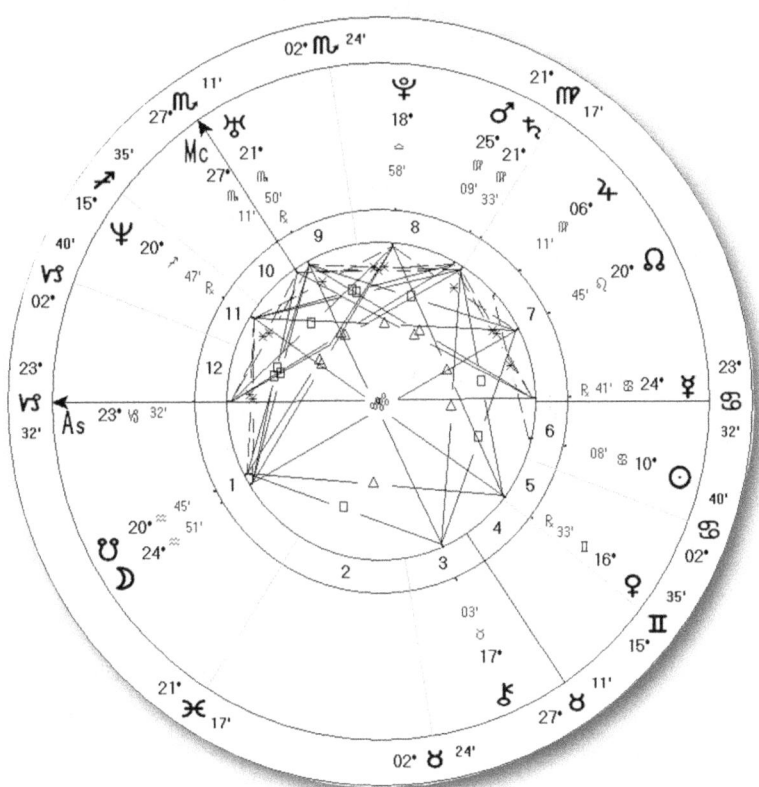

- Turn to the line on the Ephemeris that corresponds to Fred's day of birth and mark this with a small coloured dot.
- Move your finger down to the next day and call this 1981, the one after that will be 1982 and so on, until you reach the year that you want to examine, and then mark this with another small dot.
- Now note down the new planetary positions.
- You need to make some simple adjustments. For example, Fred was born late in the day, so if any of the personal planets (the Sun, Mercury, Venus or Mars) are nearing the end of a particular degree, simply push them over into the next one.
- Bear in mind that there may be planets that have turned to retrograde motion by the time you get to the progressed date. The Ephemeris will show retrograde motion. If so, give the planet(s) a backwards shove!
- The Moon will definitely have to be adjusted, because it moves a half a degree for every hour of time. Fred was born at 10pm, which is 22 hours after midnight. Half of 22 is 11, so you must add 11 degrees to the progressed Moon position.
- If you are content just to look at your subject's progressions for the time around his birthday, then leave things as they are, but if you want to work a few months backwards or forwards from the birthday, move the Moon forwards or backwards by one degree per month.
- There are various ways of recalculating the midheaven and the ascendant, and the one I describe here is the easiest and the most effective. You will have to be familiar with Raphael's Table of Houses.
- Note down the midheaven as shown on the natal chart and find it in "Raphael's Table of Houses", remembering to find the correct latitude for the place of birth.
- Count down the midheaven column a day for each year of life. The ephemeris will show midheaven positions as going from 0 degrees of a sign to 30 degrees, whereas we only go up to 29 degrees of a sign in our charts. Count everything, including the zero and the 30.
- Look across the column to find the new ascendant.
- If your subject has moved from one part of the world to another, you may want to calculate the progressed chart for the new location.

As you can see, this is do-able, but once you have done it a few times, you will definitely want to buy a program and do it on a computer. Sadly, you can usually only do progressions on pukka astrology software, and

5: Hand Calculations for Progressions

not on the cheapy programs that you can sometimes find for under £10. However, there is a quick-fix way around this, and it's simply to count a day for each year of Fred's life and then to do a natal chart for that day. For instance, if you're progressing Fred's chart to when he is thirty-five years old, count thirty-five days forward from his date of birth and make up or run off a natal chart for that day.

The following illustration shows the computer version of Fred's natal and progressed chart, with the natal chart on the inner ring and the progressed chart on the outer ring.

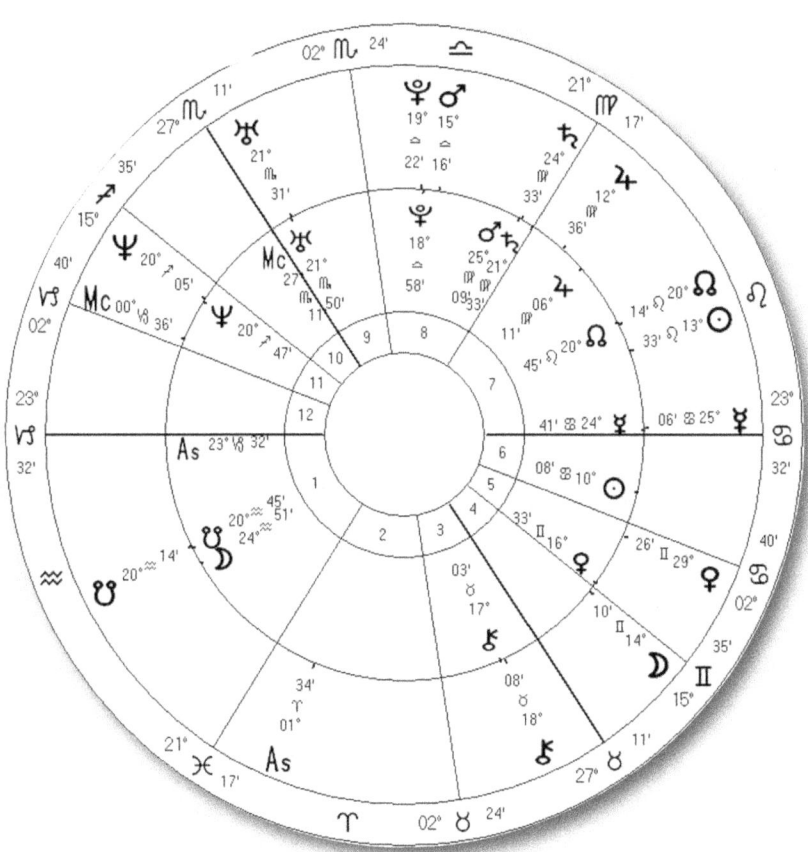

Chapter Six:
Further Methods, Ideas and Information

Here, in no particular order, are some ideas for you to examine.

Midpoints

Midpoints are the halfway point between two planets, between a planet and an angle, or between two angles. Progressions or transits to an important midpoint can be as effective as to a planet itself. If you have a computer program that lists midpoints, print out a list of them by sign and see what you have. If you have ever wondered why a particular spot on your chart seems to be sensitive to transits despite the fact that there are no planets there, a bunch of midpoints may be the answer. A good example of this is in the following natal chart, which has planets in Taurus and Gemini and then in Leo and Virgo, but nothing in Cancer. When planets traverse the sign of Cancer or work their way through the opposite sign of Capricorn, they trigger events in this person's life, due to knocking on one mid-point after another.

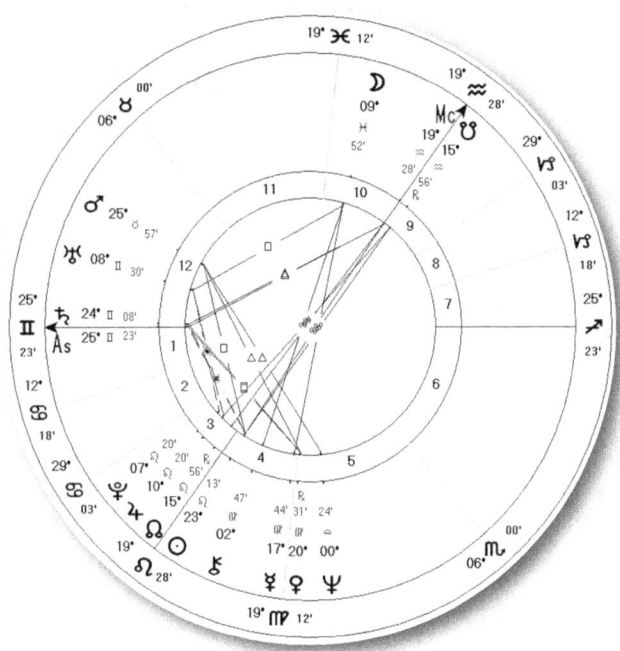

The Nodes of the Moon

The path that the Sun and the planets appear to take around our world is called the Ecliptic. The Moon's orbit around the Earth travels slightly upwards and downwards, so it crosses the ecliptic in a northerly direction and then again two weeks later in a southerly direction. The upward junction is called the North Node and the downward one is called the South Node.

Traditional Indian astrologers call the north node Rahu (the dragon's head) and the south node Kethu (the dragon's tail). Indian astrologers consider the nodes to be karmic points, with the south node showing the lessons learned in a previous life, and the north node showing what has to be learned in this one. Some western astrologers consider the north node to be those areas where a subject finds it easy to fit in with prevailing social and political circumstances.

In my experience, the nodes of the Moon link to lunar matters, particularly such things as a change of address or a major domestic upheaval. The same goes for dealings with family members, especially those concerning older female relatives. This is not to say that the karmic or social aspect of the nodes doesn't count, it is just a case of examining the subject's situation and seeing what fits. In some cases, karmic relationships seem to show up on the nodes, in other cases, matters relating to unfinished business seems to be attracted by these points, and in yet others, fame and fortune can be shown when a node is activated.

Planetoids, Asteroids and Moons

Chiron is a planetoid, asteroid or centaur, depending upon which book you read. I call it a planetoid.

You can use asteroids in astrology, if you wish. You do need to know or to look up the legends behind them before you understand them, though. Here are a few to choose from:

Amor, Ceres, Diana, Eros, Hidalgo, Icarus, Juno, Lilith, Pallas Athena, Pandora, Psyche, Sappho, Toro, Urania and Vesta.

Arabic Parts

The Arabs invented a system called "parts". Although these were principally used in natal charting to show the areas of life where a subject would succeed and be happy or where he would experience difficulties, these "parts" were also used in predictive astrology, by

6: FURTHER METHODS, IDEAS & INFORMATION

watching to see what happened when planets cross them or make other aspects to them.

The one part that has lingered on in modern astrology is the *Part of Fortune*. This is calculated from the distances in degrees between the Sun, Moon and Ascendant positions in a birthchart. The formula is not difficult, but it can be confusing:

For daytime births,
Count the number of degrees anticlockwise from the **Sun** to the **Moon**, then
Count this number, still anticlockwise, from the Ascendant.

This gives you the position of the Part of Fortune

For night time births,
Count the number of degrees anticlockwise from the **Moon** to the **Sun**, then
Count this number, still anticlockwise, from the Ascendant

This isn't as complicated as it looks, and if you are used to geometry or to using a compass, this will come easily. However, you will find the Part of Fortune is available in any decent quality astrology software these days.

When you've located your Part of Fortune, note the house that it's in, as this will show you how you will make your way in life. For instance, if it is in the Seventh house, you will make successful relationships with others. These will bring you joy, and perhaps wealth as well. If this also happens to be in the sign of Gemini or Sagittarius, you will have a lot to teach one another, and you won't run out of things to talk about with each other.

A Part of Fortune in the Second house would bring wealth, which would be personal if the sign was Aries or Taurus, or a wealthy business if it was in Capricorn.

The Vertex

The Vertex is something that I came across after writing the earlier version of this book. It is an extremely sensitive point in the chart, especially where relationship matters are concerned. If you think you might find this interesting, I have written a book about it, called "Understanding the Astrological Vertex". You definitely need a good quality software package to be able to show the Vertex.

Fixed Stars

Ancient astronomers / astrologers called stars "fixed" because they didn't appear to move around the Earth in the way that the Sun, Moon and planets did. Nowadays we know that our own Sun is a small star, close to the outer edge of a huge galaxy that we call the Milky Way. We also know that the whole galaxy is on the move and that the positions of the stars are not fixed at all. Good astrology software gives the position of the main stars and probably an interpretation of their meanings as well. There are books available that describe the fixed stars.

Just to show how "unfixed" the fixed stars actually are, the Alpha star, Regulus, moved into Virgo while I was adapting this book, after spending goodness knows how many centuries in Leo!

Chapter Seven:
The Interpretation Maze

The best way to interpret a chart is to do it logically - also to find a routine that suits you, and stick to it. Until you get so deeply into astrology that you want to experiment with unusual features, I suggest that you use the obvious features and stick to the major aspects.

From here on, it would be a good idea to get used to the common abbreviations:

The ascendant	The Asc
The midheaven	The MC
The descendant	The Dsc
The lower midheaven or nadir	The IC

Progressions and Transits

The normal day-for-a-year progressions show a fair bit of movement of the inner planets, which are the Sun, Moon, Mercury, Venus and Mars. Progressed Jupiter will have moved a little since the subject's birth, especially if the person has lived a long time, while the remaining outer planets (Saturn, Uranus, Neptune and Pluto) will have hardly moved at all. Therefore, you will probably concentrate most of your attention on the inner planets, plus the Asc and MC.

You can work through the chart planet by planet or you can start with the Asc and work your way round the chart house by house. If you work planet by planet, the following order is as good as any:

1. Asc
2. MC
3. Pluto
4. Neptune
5. Uranus
6. Saturn
7. Jupiter
8. Mars

9 Venus
10 Mercury
11 The Sun
12 Chiron
13 Nodes of the Moon
14 The Moon

I suggest that you leave the Moon to the last, because that is the planet that will take up most of your attention when doing progressions. If you decide to start with the Asc and work round, perhaps leave the Moon until last once again. We'll look more closely into the progressed Moon later in this book.

The Planetary Method in Detail

The MC

Check for changes of sign or house and any major aspect to any planet or angle because anything that affects the MC is important. After checking to see if this makes any aspects to anything on the natal chart, check to see if it makes any aspects to anything that is progressed.

The Asc

Check for everything in the same way as per the midheaven. This will probably not be as influential in its effects as the midheaven.

Pluto

This won't move enough by progression during a lifetime to be worth considering.

Neptune

This won't move enough by progression during a lifetime to be worth considering.

Uranus

Unless your subject is very old, this won't have travelled far enough to be worth considering.

7: The Interpretation Maze

Saturn
If your subject is elderly, this will be worth a glance.

Jupiter
Check for sign and house changes, aspects and retrograde motion. Check for aspects to other progressions.

Mars
Check as per Jupiter.

Venus
Check as per Jupiter.

Mercury
Check as per Jupiter.

The Sun
Check as per Jupiter. Remember that the Sun never goes retrograde.

Chiron
Check as per Jupiter.

The Nodes of the Moon
These move around the chart in retrograde motion - which means that they work their way backwards through the chart.

The Moon
This is the most important part of the whole reading, and it will probably take you as long to work through this as all the rest put together. Take your time over this.

Firstly, check to see what sign and house the Moon has progressed into. Bear in mind that the Moon moves at roughly a degree for a month, so it is easy to work out how long it has been in its current sign and house, and how much longer it will be before it changes sign or house. Look this up in the relevant chapter and also in the progressed Moon section of my book "Sasha Fenton's Moon Signs". Check out the meaning of the Moon through the signs and houses in any other predictive books you can get your hands on as well.

Now, check the actual degree of the progressed Moon and work it forward until it makes an aspect to another planet or to some other feature on the natal chart. Bear in mind that the Moon moves one degree per month.

Next, continue to move the Moon forward and check each event in turn. You may find that several months go by with nothing much happening, followed by a period when a whole bunch of aspects come hard upon each other's heels. Note down the dates and the interpretations. If you want to check that this works, try moving the Moon backwards and check what happened when it made previous aspects.

Transits

Where the transits are concerned, the situation is exactly opposite to that of the progressions. There, the outer planets hardly moved at all, so they weren't really worth bothering with, while you concentrated on the inner planets and the Moon. You will find that the inner planets and Moon move much too quickly to be of much importance, while the outer planets cause the effects.

Once again, you can run round the chart from the Asc if you prefer, or you can work planet by planet. Either way, the following will help you.

Pluto

Check for the sign and house this is in and any aspects that it makes to any planet or angle. Pluto's orbit is eccentric but very slow, so it will affect a sensitive spot on a chart for a couple of years at the very least and longer Pluto retrogrades over a particular spot. Pluto spends many years in each sign. Pluto's effect is generational as well as personal.

Neptune

When Neptune makes an aspect to a personal planet or to some other planet or feature on your chart, its effect can be felt for a couple of years. Neptune spends around twelve years in each sign.

Uranus

Uranus's effect can be felt for a year or more. Uranus spends around seven years in each sign.

Saturn

Saturn's effect can be felt for several months, sometimes up to a year. Saturn spends about two to two and a half years in each sign.

Jupiter

Jupiter's effect can be felt for a few months. Jupiter spends just over a year in each sign.

Mars

Mars's effect usually only lasts for a matter of weeks but when it is in retrograde motion, the effect will be felt for several months.

Venus

Venus transits are usually so swift that they are hardly worth bothering about but take note of those times when Venus is retrograde, because the effect will last longer and be more noticeable.

Mercury

Mercury's transits are usually to swift to bother with, but watch out for retrogrades when Mercury becomes very noticeable indeed.

The Sun

The Sun takes about a month to move through each sign, bringing the sign and house it occupies at that time into focus.

Chiron

This planetoid has an eccentric orbit but it usually spends a couple of years in a sign, therefore its transits can last for several months, especially when it turns retrograde and back again.

The Nodes of the Moon

These take about a year or so to work through each sign, so their effect can last for a few months. The Nodes move backwards through the zodiac.

The Moon

The Moon takes two and a half days to work through each sign, so its transits are very short lived. However a new Moon, a full Moon and especially an eclipse, will have a powerful effect on anything that they aspect. An eclipse that conjuncts your Sun, Moon or ascendant is always noticeable.

Some General Comments

Not all astrologers bother to use progressions, but I have always used them, and I find the progressed Moon extremely important. The fact that progressions work best for the inner planets and the transits for the outer ones means that using both methods in turn results in everything getting covered.

When I was in the early stages of working as a professional consultant, I read anything and everything I could get my hands on. Many of the books were written in the pompous, pseudo-psychological style that was in vogue in the 1970s. All the wonderful (usually American) astrologers went to great pains to explain that they prepared a pile of charts and made copious notes, well in advance of their clients actually turning up for their appointments. I came to the conclusion that they were talking through their hats, or they were extremely lucky. If I was stupid enough to prepare a chart in advance of the appointment, the client would invariably turn up and tell me that she had given me the wrong details, cheerfully announcing, "I phoned my mum this morning, and she told me that I wasn't born at three in the afternoon, but at two thirty in the morning. Does that matter?" Another popular one went, "I thought I was born in Birmingham, but it was my sister who was born there, I was actually born in Kuala Lumpur!" Very few people seem to know the difference between a.m. and p.m., and don't see that it can matter very much. I often asked a client to phone her mother or other relative from my office while she was sitting there, and I always made up the charts with the client sitting alongside me.

Oddly enough, the clients actually enjoyed watching me put their charts together. I think that it gave them a feeling that I was working on their lives and their stories in a very personal manner. I also think that sitting quietly and watching this process unfold helped them to relax, to forget the cares of the world for a while. It seemed to put them in a meditative frame of mind. It's likely that looking at their charts opened a Chakra or two in the same way that looking at Tarot cards being laid out does, and perhaps that helped me to reach into them psychically as well as astrologically!

A far more frustrating, and all too common situation, was to actually do the job and see the client happily off the premises, only to have them ring back the next day. The tentative voice on the phone saying that mum has now told her that the birth time (or date or place - or all three) was wrong! They took it very badly when I told them that if they wanted the job done again, they would have to pay for it again. They couldn't see why I should happily throw away a couple of hours of my working life due to their error. Astrologers are kindly souls who want to help their clients, but there are times when we could happily strangle them!

Oddly enough, if the birth time as given is wrong, this isn't quite the disaster in predictive work that it is in natal charting, because most of the time, you are looking at planetary movements rather than worrying too much about the nature of the person. Events are fairly easy to spot, even with a mistaken birth time.

The same goes for cases where the birth time is not known, because it is still possible to get some useful information from a "flat" or "natural" chart where your ascendant or starting point is zero degrees of Aries. In these cases, you won't have the houses to play with and the Moon position could be out by a few degrees, but it is surprising how much information you can glean out of even this kind of half-boiled job. You may even find yourself rectifying the chart and actually locating the ascendant as you go along.

The moral of all this is not to become upset when things aren't perfect, and to be prepared to "jiggle" a dodgy chart in order to get things right. Time and practice will give you a feel for this kind of work. It may also make you realise how much nicer it would be to work as a fish-gutter or a loo cleaner!

Other Types of Progressed chart

If you are dealing with a solar arc type of chart, where all the planets and other features have been moved forward by one degree, you need to find a working order that seems logical. If you want to be sure you haven't missed anything out, use the planetary order outlined earlier in this chapter and go through the planets and angles one by one.

Chapter Eight:
Progression & Transit Aspects

It makes sense to judge a progressed chart against a natal chart and check out the aspects that are formed between the two charts. If you are used to looking at planets that transit a natal chart, use the same method and the same interpretations for a progressed one. Luckily, any book that offers interpretations of the transits can be used for the progressions as well. You can use solar arc charts in exactly the same way as day-for-a-year progressions or transits.

Tip:
Solar and lunar returns, Electional charts and any kind of horary are best used as stand-alone charts.

Aspects

Progressed or transiting aspects work in the same way as natal aspects and the terminology is the same for both. The difference is that a natal aspect relates to the *character* of your subject, while progressed or transit aspects show *trends* and *events*.

Astrologers are allergic to the terms "good" and "bad", so good aspects are often referred to as being *easy* or *beneficial*, while bad ones are often called *challenging*. This kind of astrological political correctness may be irritating, but there is a good reason for it. Nothing in astrology is truly black and white and no planet or aspect can be considered to be wholly good or bad. The trick is to take into account the energies behind each planet and the modifying effects of the signs and houses that are emphasised. This sounds complicated but it soon becomes second nature.

Orbs

Astrologers have different opinions as to the size of the orbs, and there are no hard and fast rules. The table below shows the orbs that I tend to use, but when I am doing a reading, I am likely to be quite flexible about the orb, especially if some important transit or progression is involved. An aspect can often be felt coming for a long time before it actually connects on a chart, and it can fizzle out very quickly once it has passed the point of exactitude.

When a planet does a retrograde dance backwards and forwards over a sensitive point, its effects can be felt for months or even years until it finally passes away. If one planet conjoins another, retrogrades back over it and then crosses it again in a forward motion, this is called a triple conjunction. Other astrologers call a natal stellium of three planets a triple conjunction.

Symbol	Aspect	Distance (Degrees)	Orb (Degrees)
☌	Conjunction	0	8
☍	Opposition	180	8
△	Trine	120	8
□	Square	90	8
✶	Sextile	60	6
⚻	Inconjunct (quincunx)	150	6
∠	Semi-square	45	2
⚼	Sesquiquadrate	135	2
⚺	Semi-sextile	30	2
Q	Quintile	72	2
±	Bi-quintile	144	2

8: Progression & Transit Aspects

Many astrologers use tighter orbs when dealing with features such as the nodes, the Part of Fortune, the Vertex and so on. At this point in your astrological studies, I suggest that you only use the major aspects of conjunction, opposition, trine and square until you get the hang of things. Later you can add any or all the other features.

Reading the Aspects

Conjunction

This extremely powerful aspect can register a wonderful event or a nasty one depending upon the planets that are involved. You must also take into account the signs and houses in which the conjunction occurs. It is also worth noting that a conjunction in one place in a chart means that something else is being opposed, even if it is only an unoccupied house.

There is a first house feeling to a conjunction, so it always engages the attention of the subject in a very important way. Even an unpleasant conjunction usually has a good outcome in the long run.

Opposition

This is considered to be a difficult aspect, but I feel that it is where a subject has to cope with the decisions and the behaviour of others, and this doesn't have to be bad. For example, if a subject is lonely, the movement of planets into opposition to his ascendant or to something else on the chart can signal a time of meeting someone new. It is also worth noting that planets in opposition will also enhance the sign and house that they are passing through.

There is always a seventh house feeling to oppositions, and they can be quite fortunate in the long run. These progressions and transits are easier to bear if the subject understands that life is likely to be difficult while they last, and if he is prepared to learn from the experience.

Trine

This is always a pleasant, easy and rather lucky aspect, and the worst that can happen is that it goes unnoticed. A trine will set off a period of creativity, love and fun, which is in line with the fifth house feeling to which it relates. Alternatively, it can bring freedom, the chance of exploring new horizons or of learning something new in a ninth house manner.

Square

This is probably the most challenging of all aspects. In a natal chart, a square is considered to be character building, but where progressions and transits are concerned, squared planets can make the individual extremely unhappy. This may bring a fourth house feeling of investigating the roots of the matter, or a tenth house feeling of moving on and leaving something behind.

Sextile

This is a pleasant aspect that brings luck and happiness. This is supposed to be more mental and third house in character than the trine. Therefore, one would expect pleasant news or ease of communication related to the planets, signs and houses that are affected by it. This can also bring friendship, group activity, education and exploration of an eleventh house kind.

Semi-square

This can be quite difficult.

Sesquiquadrate

This is a bit challenging.

Inconjunct

Although this is a minor aspect, it is always worth considering both in natal charting and when looking at progressions and transits. It can be extremely awkward and it puts pressure on the subject, either in a kind of sixth house manner by loading him down with duties and obligations, or an eighth house manner by landing him with financial, sexual or relationship problems. The two signs involved have nothing in common, because they are of different elements and qualities. Two inconjuncts at the same time form a "yod" aspect, and this can be extremely trying.

Semi-sextile

Some astrologers see this as a pleasant aspect, rather like a minor sextile, but the signs involved aren't compatible with each other, so it may be irritating. Either way, the events involved are likely to be unremarkable.

Quintile

A quintile aspect is supposed to bestow talent, so I guess that a progressed quintile would bring talents to the fore. This is hard to spot and rarely used.

Bi-quintile
This is much the same as the Quintile, but weaker.

Parallel and Contra-Parallel Aspects
Parallel aspects form when two planets are at the same distance above or below the ecliptic. Contra-parallels form when two planets are at the same distance from the ecliptic, but one is above it while the other is below it. When it comes to interpreting both parallels and contra-parallels, consider them in the same way that you would a conjunction. Indeed, old-time astrologers reckoned that a parallel was a stronger force than a conjunction.

I suggest that if you are in the process of learning your astrology, concentrate on the ordinary major aspects such as the conjunction, sextile, square, trine and opposition, and leave the rest until later.

Progression and Transit Analysis: Susan Boyle
On the evening of the 11th of April 2009, in front of millions of people, a phenomenon occurred in the shape of Susan Boyle, when she appeared in the finals of 'Britain's Got Talent'; her singing took people's hearts by storm. So, let's start with Susan's natal chart, shown overleaf.

Mars rules the brain, and the first house rules the early stages of life, the head, the brain and the body as a whole. In Susan's case, Mars rules her Aries Sun sign. There it sits, in the first house, at the fulcrum of a T-square involving the most personal planets of all – the Sun and the Moon. Mars brought danger to her birth in the shape of oxygen starvation. This affected her brain, making her a slow-learner at school and the victim of bullies. However, this powerful angular Mars also sits at the leading edge of a grand trine to Mercury and the Neptune/Vertex conjunction, all in sensitive water signs. Susan expresses herself through music, as shown by the link between Mercury (communication) and Neptune (music) for the benefit of others (Vertex). Like many Arians and those with Mars rising, she is no raving beauty, but she has immense beauty in her voice.

Cancer rising suggests a strong bond with the parents, and that is certainly the case for Susan, as she stayed at home and cared for her parents until their death. By her own admission, she is still a virgin who has never been kissed, as shown by the dead weight of Capricorn on the seventh, eighth, and ninth house cusps, and Saturn itself sitting in the eighth house. After her parents died, a lack of opportunities for work, as well as sheer loneliness, led her into doing voluntary work for her beloved church. Neptune is well aspected and Jupiter is in her ninth house, both of which indicate benefits from religion. The heavy Saturn and Capricorn situation, especially in the eighth and ninth houses, shows a huge amount of karma in Susan's life, both in the sense of repaying some massive karmic debt and then gaining massive karmic rewards later in life. For Saturn, life truly does begin at fifty!

So, is there anything in Susan's chart to suggest fame and fortune? Susan's Cancer Asc makes her appear to outsiders as being 'mumsy' rather than anything remotely looking like a modern pop star, but Cancer is a cardinal sign, so it can make things happen when it wants to. Her Aries Sun and Libra Moon are also in cardinal signs, as are her Mars in Cancer (Mars is her Sun's ruler) and the Moon in Libra (the Moon is her chart ruler). This denotes that once she gets herself into gear, very little will stop her. When one of the nodes (preferably the north node) is conjunct Pluto, the person will achieve fame and fortune. In Susan's case, the north node is within a few seconds of an exact conjunction with Pluto.

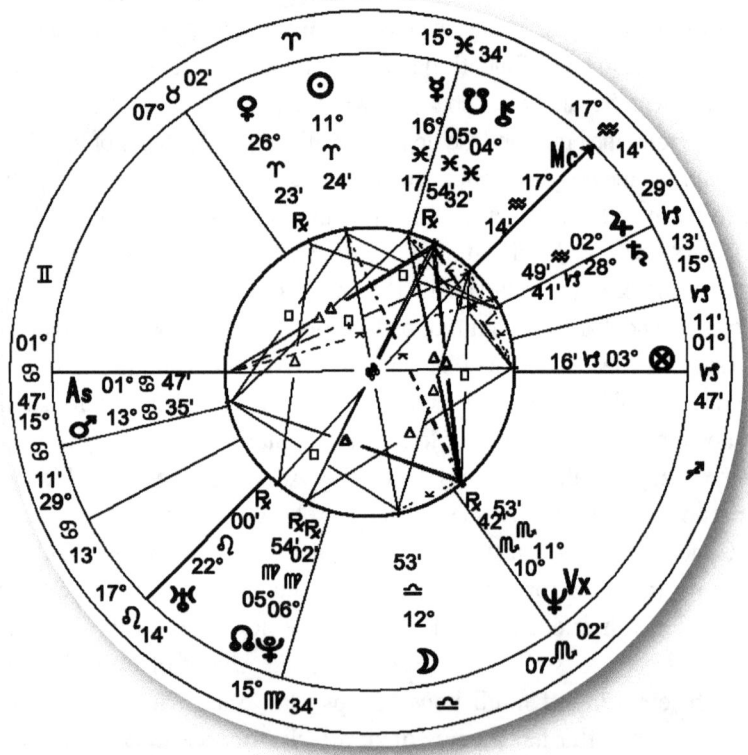

SUSAN BOYLE - NATAL CHART: 1 APRIL 1961

8: Progression & Transit Aspects

Progressions

So what happened on the fateful day? Susan has been singing for years, so she didn't do much more than she has done many times before, albeit to a larger and more important audience. My guess is that the progressions would have been more interesting when her parents died and when she started her church work; However, an Asc progressing into Leo has plenty to say about wanting to be a star, and the progressed MC shows how this slotted in for her in 2009.

- Progressed Asc into Leo.
- Progressed MC trine progressed Asc.
- Progressed MC sextile natal Jupiter.
- Progressed MC conjunct natal Sun.
- Progressed Dsc conjunct natal Jupiter and natal Saturn.

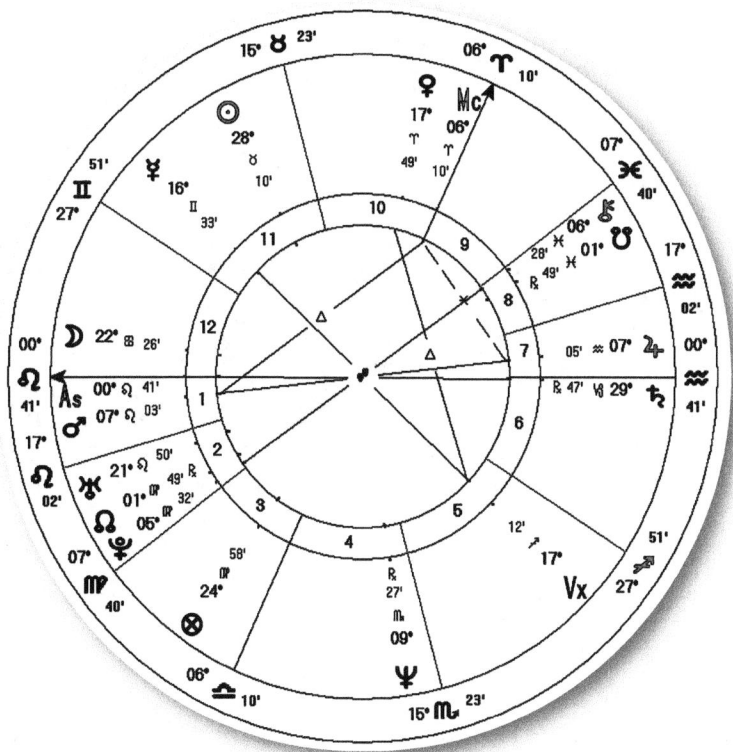

SUSAN BOYLE - PROGRESSED CHART: 8:00 P.M, 11 APRIL 2009

Transits

If some one came to me with a chart that looked like Susan's did at the time of the competition, all I could have said for certain was that the astonishing number of transiting connections showed that something extraordinary was about to occur, because when there is this much activity, it is hard to pin it down to any one thing.

It is interesting to note that, even if the show was pre-recorded, it doesn't matter much in this particular case, because the voting only took place when the show was broadcast, and it was the public's response that projected Susan into becoming a superstar.

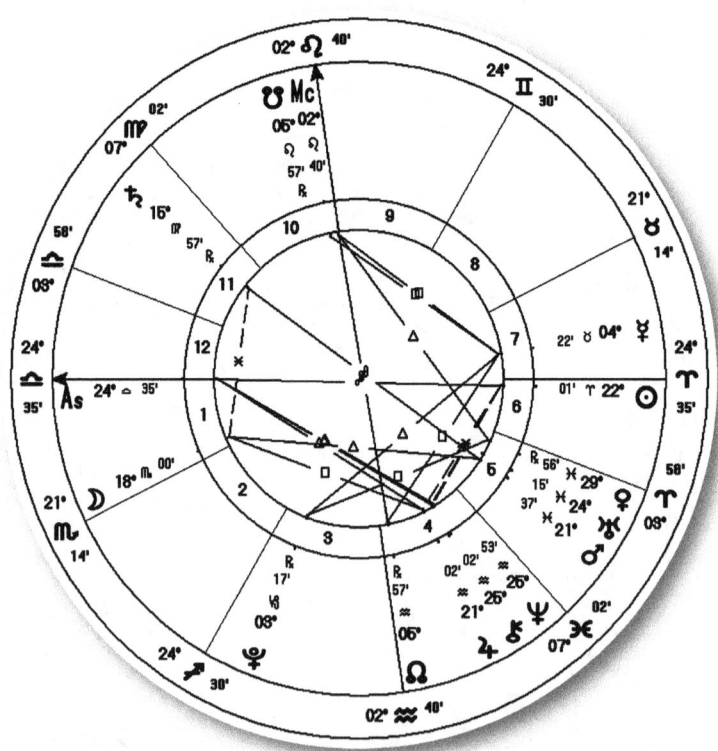

SUSAN BOYLE - TRANSIT CHART: 8:00P.M, 11 APRIL 2009

8: Progression & Transit Aspects

Here is a list of the main aspects in Susan's chart on that day:

Transiting Sun trine natal Uranus
Transiting Moon trine natal Mercury
Transiting Mercury trine natal Pluto
Transiting Mercury trine natal north node
Transiting Mercury sextile natal south node
Transiting Mercury sextile natal part of fortune
Transiting Mercury square natal Jupiter
Transiting Venus sextile natal Saturn
Transiting Mars inconjunct natal Uranus
Transiting Jupiter opposite natal Uranus
Transiting Saturn opposite natal Mercury
Transiting Saturn sextile natal Mars
Transiting Uranus sextile natal Venus
Transiting Uranus inconjunct natal Uranus
Transiting Neptune opposite natal Uranus
Transiting Neptune semi-sextile natal Saturn
Transiting Chiron semi-sextile natal Saturn
Transiting Pluto conjunct natal part of fortune (exact)
Transiting Chiron opposite natal Uranus
Transiting north node inconjunct natal north node
Transiting south node inconjunct natal south node
Transiting MC opposite natal Saturn
Transiting IC conjunct natal Saturn
Transiting MC square natal Venus
Transiting Asc opposite natal Venus

Chapter Nine:
Solar Arcs & Returns

In solar arc progressions (or directions), all the planets, along with the ascendant and midheaven, move forward at the same rate as the Sun during the course of one day, which is 57 minutes of a degree. If you are doing this by hand, simply progress everything on the chart forward by one whole degree per year and don't worry about the slight discrepancy. Write the new placements outside the natal chart.

Amazingly, solar arc progressions can be worked backwards as well as forwards! If you want to try the converse picture, push each planet backwards by one degree per year. Whether direct or converse, check for changes of sign or house or any aspects that are being made between planets, angles or anything else that looks interesting.

Solar Returns

Solar returns are a picture of the transits at the time when the Sun returns to its position at the time of a person's birth. I think these are easiest to interpret when they are read as a stand-alone chart, rather than trying to put them against a natal chart.

Solar returns are extremely difficult to do by hand, so you need decent astrology software for this. Most programs will ask you if you want the Solar return for the place of birth, or if you want to relocate the return chart to wherever the subject is living now, and you should relocate the chart.

Tip:
This is where the expression "many happy returns" comes from.

Precession

Some programs ask you if you want to take "precession" into account. Precession is a slight backwards movement of Earth that occurs over a period of time. Some astrologers use this feature, others don't. I suggest that you try both and see what works best for you.

What to Look For

The Solar return offers a flavour of the year from one birthday to the next. The most important things are the solar return Asc and MC, because these alone will tell you what kind of a year you are looking at.

If the new Asc is in Capricorn, this denotes an excellent year for work and ambition, but it may be a stressful year in which nothing comes easily.

A radical change of MC could signify a change of direction, even if only for the year in question. Otherwise, see what houses the Solar return planets fall into and generally assess the chart for the year in question. Now follow this up by working out any aspects that are formed between the solar return and the natal planets and angles.

Lunar Returns

Lunar returns are exactly the same as solar returns, but they occur every lunar month. The Moon returns to the exact position that it occupied at birth and the remaining chart is worked out around this. As this occurs every month, this will give a close up view of the month in question in the same way that the solar return does for the year in question.

The effects of the lunar return are evident from about a week before it hits until about a week afterwards. This is really quite a handy astrological tool, because so much astrology is too wide in its scope and timescale to focus itself in this way.

Chapter Ten:
Moon Phases & Eclipses

A little observation over a period of months will show you the times during each lunar month when you feel low or when you feel good. This may be down to a particular Moon phase, or a particular sign that the Moon is in. There is always a new Moon in your own Sun sign around the time of your birthday, and this may trigger the start of something new shortly after your birthday.

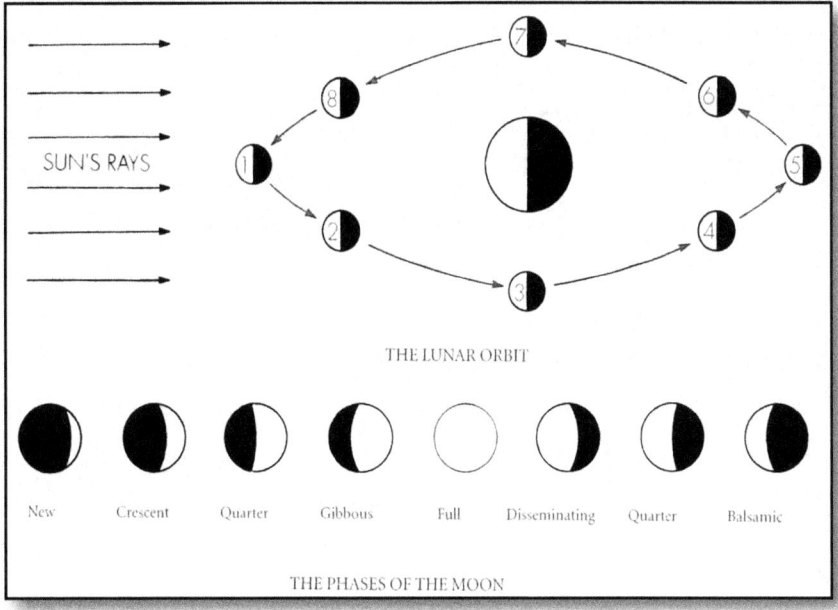

Eclipses

Eclipses occur in pairs, and at about four to five month intervals. There can be as few as three and as many as six eclipses in a year. Normally, a solar eclipse is followed by a lunar eclipse a couple of weeks later, or vice versa. Some eclipses are easy to see in the sky, but most are partial eclipses and they may only be noticeable in certain areas of the Earth.

From an astrologer's point of view, the fact that an eclipse is partial or full shouldn't make much difference, but we tend to take notice of the more spectacular ones. The Romans considered eclipses to be portents of evil, and modern astrologers tend to agree with this.

Most eclipses pass ordinary people by without notice, which is just as well, considering their frequency. However, if an eclipse falls on your Sun, Moon or Asc, you will feel its effect strongly.

If you are far enough into astrology to understand a natal chart, you may like to consider the Ptolemaic theory of eclipses:

~ An eclipse that occurs on a subject's ascendant can be felt for about three months afterwards.
~ An eclipse on the midheaven can be felt for six months afterwards.
~ An eclipse on the descendant can be felt for nine months afterwards.

My own observation is that if an eclipse occurs on a subject's Sun, Moon or Asc, he will feel it very powerfully within a couple of days, and that it will bring an unpleasant situation to a head.

Chapter Eleven:
The Cycles of Time

Wherever the planets were when a subject was born, there are times when they return to the same place. A solar return is a good example, as this happens every year on your birthday. Among the other planets, some move too quickly for their planetary return to be significant, while others move too slowly to make a return during the course of a lifetime. However, even the slowest planet will move a quarter or a third of the way around the chart, sparking off events as they pass any tender spots on the birthchart.

All planets have slight variations in their orbits from time to time, and all except the Sun and Moon appear to travel backwards from time to time. Astrologers call this backwards movement retrograde motion.

The Planetary Cycles

The Earth orbits the Sun in approximately 365.25 days (one year).
The Moon orbits the Earth in 27.5 days.
Mercury orbits the Sun in 88 days.
Venus orbits the Sun in 225 days.
Mars orbits the Sun in 1 year 10.5 months.
Jupiter orbits the Sun in 12 years.
Saturn orbits the Sun in 29 years.
Uranus orbits the Sun in 84 years.
Neptune orbits the Sun in 165 years.
Pluto orbits the Sun in 246 years.
Chiron orbits the Sun in roughly 51 to 52 years.

There is absolutely no need for you to memorise these cycles, but there are a few that will become familiar. A point worth bearing in mind is that these cycles affect everybody. If you mix with other astrologers, you will soon become used to the terms "the Saturn return", or the "Uranus half-return".

The Planetary Movements in Detail

The Moon

The Moon travels around the Earth once each month, so there will be one day in every 27.5 days when it returns to the place that it was when a subject was born. This is called a lunar return.

The Earth

From an astrologer's point of view, the Earth stands still while the Sun, Moon and planets orbit round us. We know that this isn't the case, but for the time being, let us assume that the Earth is the centre of the Solar system rather than the Sun.

The Sun

From our perspective on Earth, the Sun appears to move through the whole zodiac once a year. A Solar return is the time when the Sun returns to the position it occupied when you were born. It is often the case that the solar return tends to fall on a day before or after your birthday. This is usually a sociable and happy time.

Mercury

Mercury moves very quickly and it is never far from the Sun. In common with all the other planets, (except the Sun and Moon), there are times when it appears to be moving backwards! The term is Retrograde Motion. Mercury's return occurs once a year, around the time of your birthday. This is a time for thinking and for making plans.

Venus

Venus moves more slowly than Mercury, but it is also never far from the Sun. About once a year, it will spend some time in retrograde motion. However, Venus usually returns to its own place at around birthday time. Venus's return will make you take some time to review your financial and relationship situations. It often sparks off a period of socialising, the desire for a holiday or a bit of luxury.

Mars

A Mars return occurs once every 1 year and 10.5 months. A Mars return can set off noticeable changes, but the outcome will depend upon the

11: The Cycles of Time

signs, houses and aspects that are involved. A return for a Mars that is natally in the twelfth house will bring a great boost to one's psychic powers, while simultaneously bringing some kind of health setback. This is due to this powerful return occurring opposite the sixth house of health. A Mars return in the first house will boost health, confidence and general lifestyle, but it may have a murderous effect on relationships (seventh house).

Because Mars is one of the speedier planets, the effects of its returns, half-returns and other aspects are usually over fairly quickly.

Jupiter

Jupiter takes twelve years to make its return. You should take into account the sign and the house that natal Jupiter occupies, as well as any planets that aspect Jupiter natally when looking at this return. Jupiter is a bit of a double-edged sword; astrology books tell us that Jupiter is "the great benefic", or a planet that bestows all kinds of goodies upon its subjects. Alas, this is not quite the case. You may remember reading that the old Roman god, Jupiter (or Jove, if you prefer), tossed down thunderbolts from Mount Olympus whenever he was out of sorts. Therefore, a Jupiter return can bring sudden and unpleasant changes into a subject's life, but they usually work out for the best in the long run. If the subject loses something or someone from his life under a Jupiter return, it is probably no bad thing.

Jupiter returns at the ages of 12, 24, 36, 48, 60, 72, 84 and 96. At these times, you can expect to form good friendships with people who share your beliefs and outlook on life. You may start a career, find a mate, make a home, give life to a child or find your feet in some way at these times, and you should find something to believe in.

Jupiter half-returns occur at the following ages: 6, 18, 30, 42, 54, 66, 78, 80 and 92.

These can be times of setback and loss, but even so, they shouldn't be too troublesome.

Saturn

This is the planet that all astrologers mutter about darkly, because the Saturn returns at the ages of 29/30 and 57/59 can take a lot of living through. Oddly enough, these hard times can ultimately bring great benefits in their wake, because they set up challenges that bring terrific rewards. The easiest way to understand Saturn's effects is to see them in the form of a table, as shown below.

Tip:
The trines and sextiles vary in their timing as we get older.

The Saturn Cycle		
Age	Aspect	Probable Effect
7/8	Square	Sadness, loss, realisation that life is not all fun and games.
14/15	Opposition (half return)	Responsibilities begin to weigh heavily. Possible family problems.
19/20	Trine	Often a good time, although extra responsibility is often sought and there may be disappointments.
29/30	Return	Taking responsibility for one's own life. Realising what one really wants to do. Marriage, divorce, parenthood.
37/38	Square	Extra work challenges or other responsibilities may be sought. Women may realise that the biological clock is ticking away.
44/45	Opposition	Middle age. End of childbearing and of some career possibilities. Health may be less reliable.
52/53	Square	The last real thrust towards major work ambitions can be made at this time. Sometimes, the end of a troublesome relationship or serious health issues.
57/59	Return	Health may be an issue. Retirement may beckon. Financial setbacks are possible. May realise that something needs to be dropped for good.

11: THE CYCLES OF TIME

Uranus

The orbit of Uranus is 82 to 84 years. Uranus is the "breakout" planet, bringing issues of freedom and originality to the fore. If you have lived the same kind of life for years, you may kick over the traces when Uranus is active in your life. The outcome will vary according to the sign and house that Uranus is in at birth, and it will be modified by any other planetary aspects that may be involved. From now on, whenever you read your newspaper, take a mental note of the ages of those people who suddenly lose their cool and do strange things, as the chances are that they are being influenced by the good old "Uranus half".

Oddly enough, astrologers don't seem to take much notice of the Uranus squares that occur at 21 and 63, but these also force a subject to reappraise his life, and to make what appear to be sudden and unexpected changes. Astrological theory tells us that squares are challenging, but they aren't always bad. They mark the times when we make decisions based on what has gone before and what we want from the future.

All these outer planets have fairly eccentric orbits, so it is only worth looking in any detail at the aspects that they make against specific, individual birthcharts.

Neptune

Roughly speaking, the good times should occur at around the age of 28 and 52, while the worst times should be at around 42 and 83, give or take a year or two either way. The best aspects of Neptune bring love, unconditional friendship, spiritual happiness, an outburst of artistic or creative talent and an appreciation of the finer things of life. The bad times may bring sadness, strange health problems, confusion and a loss of faith in everything.

Pluto

Pluto's orbit is so eccentric that is has to be looked at against each individual birthchart.

Ages of Change

The following table will make it easy to spot the major times of change in everyone's life. Remember that the planets move at a slightly different rate for different age groups, so be flexible when looking at this list.

Age	Planetary Movement
7	Saturn square natal Saturn.
12	Jupiter return.
14	Saturn opposite natal Saturn (Saturn half-return).
18	Jupiter opposite natal Jupiter (Jupiter half-return).
21	Saturn square natal Saturn.
24	Jupiter return.
29/30	Saturn return.
30	Jupiter opposite natal Jupiter.
36	Saturn square natal Saturn. Jupiter return.
39/42	Uranus opposite natal Uranus (Uranus half-return).
42	Neptune square natal Neptune.
42	Jupiter opposite natal Jupiter.
44	Saturn opposite natal Saturn.
48	Jupiter return.
51	Saturn square natal Saturn.
57/58	Saturn return.
60	Jupiter return.
63	Uranus square natal Uranus.
66	Saturn square natal Saturn.
72	Jupiter return.
75	Saturn opposite natal Saturn.
80	Saturn square natal Saturn.
80/84	Uranus return.
84	Jupiter return.

11: THE CYCLES OF TIME 55

A very nice couple, Bruno and Louise Huber used to practice astrology in their native country, Switzerland. Sadly, they are both dead now. They looked at astrology with fresh eyes, and came up with several revolutionary ideas; for instance, they decided that Saturn ruled the mother in a person's chart, as it was usually she who laid down the rules in a household, and disciplined the children. The father was represented by the loving Moon in their system.

A second feature was the way they viewed aspects in a natal chart, as they not only took their meaning from the type of aspect (e.g. sextile, square, etc.), but also by the visual shapes the aspects made on a chart. They categorised a large variety of shapes, especially various triangles, into specific meanings. If you are at all interested in examining this variety of astrological systems, search for the Huber System on the Internet.

However, it is yet another highly idiosyncratic "Huberism" that I want to show you here, and that involves the Huber Jupiter Cycle and Half Cycle. This actually left Jupiter behind and became a kind of numerological system, because what you have to do is mentally run through your life, noting the changes that you made or that overtook you every six years. The list may look something like this:

~ Age 6 Moving from reception class to proper school.
~ Age 12 Change to secondary school, also the beginning of puberty.
~ Age 18 College starts, the brain "grows"; maybe the start of a career.
~ Age 24 Could be a serious relationship or the start of parenthood.
~ Age 30 End of youth, responsibilities loom, often marriage, divorce, parenthood, or finding a better career.
~ Age 36 Often a decision to have a/another child or to have no more children, therefore sterilisation. Career gets serious.
~ Age 42 Change of job, opening a business, remarriage, second family, or new child on the way.
~ etc, etc, etc

The weird thing is that this seems to work well, and it marks the passages in many people's lives.

Chapter Twelve:
Recap: The Right Method for Each Job

The previous chapter was designed to show you what the various forms of progression are and how they work, while this one looks at various techniques available to you, and each one's intended purpose.

Transits

This is the most common predictive method of all. Transits can be used to look at any aspect of life, and they are also useful when you want to focus on a specific period of time.

Day-for-a-Year Progressions

This method gives a good overview of a subject's situation and it also gives plenty of specific information. The Moon is the thing to watch, because it shows the general mood and outlook of the subject at the time of the reading and it moves quickly enough by progression for an astrologer to pick out special events. Do the progressions and then use the transits against both the natal and progressed for the best results.

Solar Arc Directions

This is useful for a general look at a subject's life. Try looking at the progressed midheaven and the progressed Sun. I have never used transits against this method but there is no reason why you shouldn't.

Tertiary, Minor and Duodenary Progressions and the Ninety-Degree Arc Method

Experiment with these if you like. I've never used them commercially.

Solar Returns and Lunar Returns

The Solar returns can be used to focus on a particular situation or on life in general, and they give a wonderful flavour of a particular year. Lunar returns give an even closer look, as they show the situation in a particular month.

Venusian and Martian Arcs

Leave these on Venus and Mars!

Decumbitures

If you like horary astrology, you will love Decumbitures. Use these to analyse and diagnose an illness. This is a great aid to astrological herbalists and other health workers. You need to be fully conversant with all aspects of Decumbitures before diagnosing anything.

Horary Astrology

Ask yourself a question, such as "Will I get the job I am going after?" Make up a chart for the time the question is asked and see if it answers it. This is best for those who have thoroughly studied this technique, as the rules and terminology in horary are different to "standard" astrology.

Electional Astrology

This allows you to find the best time to do something important. Try making up a chart of the time and date you think is right as if it were a natal chart, and then judge its chances of success.

Mundane Astrology

This is the astrology of towns, cities, politics and so on. Try finding the chart for a specific country or a political party and work out what is likely to happen to it over the next six months.

Daily House Progressions and the Perpetual Noon Date

Don't bother with these methods.

Chapter Thirteen:
Astrology and the Body

Check out the following list to see how the signs, houses and planets link to the different parts of the body. This list will come in very handy when you want to check out the state of health on a progressed chart of any kind. The information here is too basic for those who want to make a career of medical astrology, but it is good enough for the rest of us.

Engage your brain before opening your mouth when dealing with this facet of astrology, because the last thing you want to do is to alarm anyone, or to plant the idea in someone's head that they are likely to become ill.

Aries, First House, Mars

Part of body
The head, brain, eyes, skull and upper jaw. Pineal gland, arteries to the head and brain.
Potential ailments
Headaches, acne, fainting, neuralgia, fevers of the brain, blindness.

Taurus, Second House, Venus

Part of body
The lower jaw, the throat - including the thyroid gland, the neck, larynx, chin, ears, tongue, vocal chords, upper (cervical) spine, jugular vein and tonsils.
Potential ailments
Laryngitis, throat inflammation, over/under-active thyroid, tonsillitis and goitre.

Gemini, Third House, Mercury

Part of body
The upper respiratory system, the shoulders, arms, wrists, hands, fingers and upper ribs.
Potential ailments
Bronchitis, asthma, chest disorders, accidents to arms, shoulders and hands. Also the nervous system and the mind.

Cancer, Fourth House, the Moon
Part of body
The lungs, breasts, rib cage, stomach and digestive organs, alimentary canal, sternum, womb and pancreas.
Potential ailments
Gastric disorders, heartburn, diabetes and obesity.

Leo, Fifth House, the Sun
Part of body
The spine - especially the upper back, spinal cord, heart, arteries - especially the aorta, circulation, spleen.
Potential ailments
Back complaints, spinal meningitis, and heart diseases.

Virgo, Sixth House, Mercury & Chiron
Part of body
The lower digestive system, the bowels, the lower dorsal nerves, the skin, nervous system and the mind.
Potential ailments
Bowel diseases, indigestion, colic, intestinal infection. Skin infections and nervous or stress-related disorders. Let us not forget hypochondria!

Libra, Seventh House, Venus
Part of body
The bladder, kidneys, lumbar region, haunches to buttocks, adrenal glands, lumbar nerves, blood vessels.
Potential ailments
Kidney and bladder disorders, eczema, lumbago, abscesses.

Scorpio, Eighth House, Pluto & Mars
Part of body
The reproductive and sexual organs - especially the cervix, lower stomach, lower spine including the coccyx, groin, anus, genitourinary system, prostate gland - and the eyes.
Potential ailments
Bladder disorders, genitourinary diseases, prostate or menstrual problems, piles.

13: ASTROLOGY AND THE BODY

Sagittarius, Ninth House, Jupiter
Part of body
The hips and thighs, pelvis, sacrum, the liver, the sciatic nerve, the arterial system - especially the femoral artery.
Potential ailments
Injuries and diseases of hips, thighs and pelvis. Sciatica, liver disorders, paralysis of limbs.

Capricorn, Tenth House, Saturn
Part of body
The skin, ears, teeth, bones, knees and bones above and below the knees.
Potential ailments
Chronic ailments of any kind. Rheumatism, skin complaints, knee injuries, bone diseases.

Aquarius, Eleventh House, Uranus & Saturn
Part of body
The ankles, calves, shins, breathing, circulatory system - especially to the extremities.
Potential ailments
Calf and ankle injuries, varicose veins, poor circulation, blood diseases, heart palpitations.

Pisces, Twelfth House, Neptune & Jupiter
Part of body
The feet and toes, lungs, lymphatic system and pituitary gland.
Potential ailments
Bunions, chilblains, tendonitis in the feet, drink and drug problems, lymphatic and glandular disorders. Also allergies and strange psychic phenomena.

Chapter Fourteen:
Signs of the Zodiac

By now, you can see that predictive astrology depends upon a static natal chart, around which (progressed / transiting) planets and other features move, making beneficial or difficult aspects to the natal planets and features as they travel along. However, everything that happens on a horoscope chart also has to move through the signs of the zodiac, and a planet will work differently when moving through one sign, than in the next.

For instance, the Sun rules the fire sign of Leo, so it's happiest when passing through the fire signs of Aries, Leo and Sagittarius. It's reasonably happy when in the air signs of Gemini, Libra and Aquarius, uncomfortable in the earth signs of Taurus, Virgo and Capricorn, and unhappy in the water signs of Cancer, Scorpio and Pisces.

The same concept goes for all the other planets. For example, Saturn is associated with the cardinal earth sign of Capricorn, and the fixed air sign of Aquarius, so Saturn can find something to work with in cardinal signs, fixed signs, earth signs, air signs, or the decans that link to Capricorn and Aquarius. It is also comfortable in Libra, where ancient astrology tells us it is "exalted". The lists below show the various ways in which the signs can be divided up and described.

The Genders

Masculine signs are quick and assertive, while feminine ones have more endurance.

Aries	Masculine
Taurus	Feminine
Gemini	Masculine
Cancer	Feminine
Leo	Masculine
Virgo	Feminine
Libra	Masculine
Scorpio	Feminine

Sagittarius Masculine
Capricorn   Feminine
Aquarius   Masculine
Pisces   Feminine

The Elements

The signs divide into four elements of fire, earth, air and water. The fire signs are enthusiastic and quick, the air signs are thinkers, the earth signs get things done while the water signs make good use of intuition and empathy.

Aries   Fire
Taurus   Earth
Gemini   Air
Cancer   Water
Leo   Fire
Virgo   Earth
Libra   Air
Scorpio   Water
Sagittarius Fire
Capricorn   Earth
Aquarius   Air
Pisces   Water

The Qualities

The signs divide into three qualities of cardinal, fixed and mutable. The cardinal signs take charge, the fixed signs finish what they start and the mutable signs move things along.

Aries   Cardinal
Taurus   Fixed
Gemini   Mutable
Cancer   Cardinal
Leo   Fixed
Virgo   Mutable
Libra   Cardinal
Scorpio   Fixed
Sagittarius Mutable
Capricorn   Cardinal
Aquarius   Fixed
Pisces   Water

14: SIGNS OF THE ZODIAC

Decans

Each sign of the zodiac can be divided into three decans. Each sign contains 30 degrees and each decan comprises ten degrees, the first of which repeats the sign itself, while the second and third decans follow along in the same element. This will make sense when you look at the list below:

The Fire Signs

Aries
First decan   Aries
Second decan   Leo
Third decan   Sagittarius

Leo
First decan   Leo
Second decan   Sagittarius
Third decan   Aries

Sagittarius
First decan   Sagittarius
Second decan   Aries
Third decan   Leo

The Earth Signs

Taurus
First decan   Taurus
Second decan   Virgo
Third decan   Capricorn

Virgo
First decan   Virgo
Second decan   Capricorn
Third decan   Taurus

Capricorn
First decan   Capricorn
Second decan   Taurus
Third decan   Virgo

The Air Signs
Gemini
First decan	Gemini
Second decan	Libra
Third decan	Aquarius

Libra
First decan	Libra
Second decan	Aquarius
Third decan	Gemini

Aquarius
First decan	Aquarius
Second decan	Gemini
Third decan	Libra

The Water Signs
Cancer
First decan	Cancer
Second decan	Scorpio
Third decan	Pisces

Scorpio
First decan	Scorpio
Second decan	Pisces
Third decan	Cancer

Pisces
First decan	Pisces
Second decan	Cancer
Third decan	Scorpio

The Ancient Divisions
The following table comes from older forms of astrology. Some astrologers love these divisions and use them all the time, while others ignore them. Purists would normally only include those planets that can be seen with the naked eye, but some astrologers now include the distant planets, albeit with some dispute over the signs they affect.

14: Signs of the Zodiac

PLANET	RULERSHIP	EXALTATION	DETRIMENT	FALL
Sun	Leo	Aries	Aquarius	Libra
Moon	Cancer	Taurus	Capricorn	Scorpio
Mercury	Gemini & Virgo	Virgo	Sagittarius & Pisces	Pisces
Venus	Taurus & Libra	Pisces	Aries & Scorpio	Virgo
Mars	Aries & Scorpio	Capricorn	Taurus & Libra	Cancer
Jupiter	Sagittarius & Pisces	Cancer	Gemini & Virgo	Capricorn
Saturn	Capricorn & Aquarius	Libra	Cancer & Leo	Aries
Uranus	Aquarius	Scorpio	Leo	Taurus
Neptune	Pisces	Cancer & Leo	Virgo	Capricorn & Aquarius
Pluto	Scorpio	Aries & Pisces	Taurus	Virgo & Libra

Chapter Fifteen:
The Sun through the Signs & Houses

It would be lovely to explore every possible progression in detail by examining its effects on the psychology of the subject, looking into all the things that could happen and giving countless examples, but this book isn't big enough, so I'll simply explore the essence of each progression or transit.

The Sun

By day-for-a-year progression, the Sun spends thirty years traversing a sign and it will take the same time to cross a house if you use the equal house method. The Sun takes a month by transit to cross a sign or an equal house by transit. The Sun never travels retrograde.

Tip:
The Sun corresponds to the fifth house and Leo

Character

Solar progressions and transits always denote important experiences. In theory, this should affect the public aspects of a subject's life, rather than personal feelings or domestic and family matters. Beneficial aspects can bring success in any area of life, happiness in connection with children, holidays, amusements and a fun-filled love life. Adverse aspects can bring great suffering and hardship, but these can be character building and much can be learned from them. Spiritual lessons may have to be learned at such times. The Sun is at its most comfortable and effective when traversing any of the fire signs, whether by transit or progression. The Sun is fairly compatible with air signs, but less so with earth signs and least comfortable when journeying through water signs.

Where to Start

Start by looking at the sign that the Sun is in, then look at the house and then check out the decan. Don't rush: take your time.

The Sun through Aries or the First House

You have reached the end of a phase and are now ready to start something new. New ideas, aims ambitions, renewed energy and a "kick-start" can be applied to your life. There will be satisfaction from looking back over what has been done in the past, but also impatience to get on with the new phase. You will gradually notice yourself becoming more outgoing and Arian in nature. You could start to take an interest in Arian jobs, such as teaching, social work, the armed forces or other large organisations, and you may take up hobbies such as engineering or making things.

Beneficial aspects to the Sun open the doors of opportunity. This would be a good time to seek favours, promotion, advancement and to deal with superiors. Challenging aspects could bring illness, a lack of energy, trouble at work and a loss of position or prestige. Difficult aspects can also bring great benefits, but these will be hard won.

The Sun through Taurus or the Second House

Movement into this sign or house exerts a calming influence and makes you less impulsive, less apt to take up sudden enthusiasms, while growing more reliable and sensible instead. If you have been a bit footloose up to now, you will soon settle into a job and family life, and make as much of a go of it as possible. You will be more stubborn and you may develop a stick-in-the mud attitude but you will also be more inclined to put down roots. Your life will be less eventful, but anything that does occur will be more profound.

Your attitude will be friendly and sociable and you may take up creative Taurean hobbies such as gardening, the fashion trade, building and cooking. You will need to guard against developing a sweet tooth and giving yourself a weight problem. You make an effort to obtain and to keep money and possessions.

You will search for and find your own value system, if necessary, rejecting that of your parents and schoolteachers. Beneficial aspects to the Sun in this sign or house bring money, property and goods. These

15: THE SUN THROUGH THE SIGNS & HOUSES

also bring beauty, harmony and comfort. Challenging ones can temporarily remove these things or make them harder to obtain.

The Sun through Gemini or the Third House
When the Sun moves into this sign or house, you will want to give up some of your more materialistic ways in favour of a more intellectual approach. You will be happy to study and to pass on information to others and you will become more perceptive and critical. Life will hold more variety and you will be more versatile, dexterous, brighter but also more restless.

Local travel will become more important and there will be much contact with neighbours, siblings and colleagues. When the Sun is well aspected, negotiations, intellectual pursuits and contacts with others will progress well. Under challenging aspects, these things will prove to be a struggle but intellectual and other benefits can accrue as a result of efforts being made.

The Sun through Cancer or the Fourth House
When the Sun progresses into this sign or house, you will be less of a rolling stone and more of a stable family person. You could set up a home, open a small business or become more involved with the members of your family under this influence. You may feel more attached to your mother and to other older women.

History and the past will begin to fascinate you and you could start to collect things that have some special meaning for you. This isn't a particularly comfortable placement for the Sun, because your feelings are made more sensitive and painful.

Easy aspects will bring luck with property, family matters and any work that is carried out in the home. Difficult aspects could disrupt these elements of life and or make it hard to achieve a happy family life. The feelings could be very tender when tough aspects occur.

The Sun through Leo or the Fifth House
This being the Sun's natural sign or house, it is at its best here. You should become more centred, happier about yourself and about your way of life. You will be more egotistic or arrogant, but also more successful in everything you do, so you will probably deserve the right become somewhat insufferable! You will become a more powerful figure and you

will be happy to display any extra wealth, extra goodies, talents or anything else that you gain under this influence.

You may become concerned with the things attached to this sign or house, such as creative work, show business, dealing with children and young people or working in the leisure industry. Your attitude to business will be less cautious and more flamboyant and entrepreneurial.

Under beneficial aspects, you can reach for the stars and get just about anything that you want from life but, under difficult ones, you could lose most of your gains - for a while at least. However, you won't stay down for long and your optimistic mood will soon return.

The Sun through Virgo or the Sixth House
When the Sun reaches this sign or house, you become more diligent and more concerned with the needs of others. You will quieten down and get your head down in order to concentrate on details. Detailed work such as computing, dressmaking and astrology might appeal. You will be less arrogant and more modest, less confident and outgoing and more cautious. In some ways, life becomes harder.

You may become interested in sixth house matters such as, health and healing. You may also feel the urge to take up issues that are attached to the terms and conditions of other people's employment. You may take on voluntary work in a hospital or a trades union. Try to keep your confidence level high by avoiding negative or critical people and try to avoid criticising yourself too much.

Another problem area is the Virgo habit of destroying anything that looks as if it is likely to be successful before it really materialises. Under beneficial aspects, you will turn into a good employer or employee and you will also make money and learn how to keep it. Under challenging aspects, health or business setbacks can occur.

The Sun through Libra or the Seventh House
This connects you to other people and makes you less self-centred or self-reliant. Marriage, partnerships and working partnerships become important now and you may find a partner, split from someone or make changes within working partnerships. If you have any enemies, they will come out into the open. You will look at value systems that are different from those that you grew up with and you will strive to put your life into balance again.

15: THE SUN THROUGH THE SIGNS & HOUSES   73

Libran jobs and interests may attract you, possibly leading you to take up a career as an agent or a go-between. Issues of justice and fair play also begin to play a role, and you will want to fight for what you think is right. You may have to get involved in legal dealings, either in connection with work or as a result of changes in your personal life. You will become more laid back, lazier and less interested in harsh reality. Under beneficial aspects, marriage, partnerships and work arrangements all do well while under challenging aspects; these spheres of life can become difficult. He may have to fight off enemies.

The Sun through Scorpio or the Eighth House
This planetary movement will make you stronger and more positive about everything that you do and you may even be quite earnest and humourless at times. You will be less inclined to sit back and let things happen or to rely upon others. Psychic or spiritual matters could begin to attract you and issues of life and death with both fascinate you. You may be personally affected by life and death situations.

Guard against becoming despotic, too ambitious or disinclined to take the feelings of others into account. You may take up a job that involves probing or investigating. Possibilities might be surgery, oil exploration, insurance fraud investigation, forensic work, mining and so on. You will deal with legacies, mortgages, divorce settlements, shares and anything else that connects money to yourself and others.

Sex and sexual relationships will become a strong force in your life now and this itself could lead to a firm commitment to new way of life. The key idea here is of merging yourself or your money with others. Under beneficial aspects, you will gain from the some of the above-mentioned ideas and you will receive karmic benefits. Under challenging aspects, problems arise and there may be karmic debts to be repaid. Resentment and even hatred might become a problem now.

The Sun through Sagittarius or the Ninth House
The ninth house and Sagittarius are considered "lucky", and the Sun is comfortable in a fire sign. You will feel the urge to expand your mental, physical and philosophical horizons in a number of ways. There will be a strong desire to break away and to increase your personal freedom. You may travel to distant places, and contacts with people from other lands and backgrounds will become important. You may work in an

import/export business and it is even possible that you decide to take up with a foreigner.

Religion, philosophy and the spiritual side of life will start to interest you and you may discover that you have hidden talents as a medium, a healer or even an astrologer. Some people learn a lot about the law under this influence, either through their work or through personal circumstances. Teaching and learning begin to interest you. The most important issue is that you will be forced to examine your beliefs in the hunt for a philosophy of life that works for you. Under beneficial aspects, all the ideas mentioned above would prosper, while under difficult ones, you will find your beliefs challenged and your attempts to expand your mental, physical and spiritual horizons being stifled. There could be legal problems. Guard against attacking those who don't mean you any harm.

The Sun through Capricorn or the Tenth House
You will begin to reach for the top now, becoming more ambitious and serious in your attitudes. This sign and house are very much associated with banking, finance and big business so these will become an important part of your life. You will seek financial security, roots and status and this will lead to a more materialistic attitude.

Politics, publicity and prominence would all become important now. You could become more attached to your parents; especially a father or father figure at this time, and you will have more sympathy with older people in general. Under beneficial aspects, you reach the top of the heap but under difficult ones, you would fall from grace. Guard against becoming coldly ambitious at the expense of fun or of your personal relationships.

The Sun through Aquarius or the Eleventh House
When the Sun moves into this sign or house, you won't be any less ambitious but your goals will be different. Your outlook will be less self-centred and more universal. You will take an interest in humanitarian or environmental issues or any number of other causes. Groups of like-minded people will appeal and you may become involved with unions, local or national governments.

You will be interested in studying and also teaching, and for some of you social work will appeal. Astrology and other philosophical systems

15: THE SUN THROUGH THE SIGNS & HOUSES

will interest you and you will become less conventional and more eccentric as time progresses.

Guard against obstinacy and too independent an attitude and utilise the other Aquarian traits, such as, friendliness and helpfulness. Don't allow idealism to make you lose touch with reality. Under favourable aspects, you will be happy, outgoing and fulfilled while, under challenging ones, you could feel isolated and up against it. Avoid becoming eccentric, dogmatic and difficult.

The Sun through Pisces or the Twelfth House
You become kinder and more spiritual under this sign. You probably won't give up worldly ambitions and become a hermit, but there is bound to be a more introspective attitude. You will be more sensitive to others and much more interested in psychic or spiritual matters.

Circumstances may push you into giving up some aspect of your life and to become more self-sacrificial in some way. You may choose or you may be forced to live part of your life in seclusion for a while. This may be the result of karmic debts that need to be repaid.

On a practical level, you will enjoy working on creative or artistic projects and you may learn to play a musical instrument. You could also travel in connection with your work. Under favourable aspects, artistic, creative, musical, poetic or spiritual matters will prosper. Mysterious events could occur that bring help and guidance from strange sources. Under distressing aspects, you will be lonely.

Chapter Sixteen:
The Moon through the Signs and Houses

Ensure that you learn how to read the progressed Moon, because this gives a marvellous picture of the circumstances that a subject is living through at a specific time. This will show what is occupying his mind at the time of the reading.

The Moon takes about two-and-a-half years to progress through a sign (roughly a degree per month). If the equal house method is used, the Moon also takes two-and-a-half years to pass through each house. If Placidus, Koch or any other method is used, the Moon could take anything from less than a year to about four years to pass through a house. While I'm on the subject of house systems, I suggest that you use whatever system you like for natal charting, but, if you are a beginner, stick to the equal house method when doing predictive astrology, because it is easier. As it happens, I prefer the equal house method for predictive work, as it seems to be more accurate than other systems.

A lunar transit will pass by in a matter of hours, but it can be extremely useful when looking at a very critical event that occurs at a specific time. Typical examples would be signing a contract, attending a job interview or making an important phone call.

Tip:
The Moon corresponds to the fourth house and to the sign of Cancer.

Character
The Moon refers to personal and inner, emotional matters and also the atmosphere closely surrounding the subject. Domestic and family circumstances are important and when the Moon is activated by transit or progression, the individual will be forced to make an evaluation of his or her family and personal life. Petty and unimportant matters may take on a large significance for a while and then subside quickly once the progression has passed. Mothers, motherhood and women in general are

ruled by the Moon, as are a whole collection of strange things, such as dealing with the public, travel and restlessness, and health matters that are brought on by stress. Sometimes odd things surface, such as dealings with the sea, sailors, fishing, sewing and cooking.

The Moon can bring out the character of a planet, angle, sign or house when it progresses over or through it, because it reflects the energies from the other features on the chart rather than stamping its own nature on them. Where events are concerned, the Moon really does act as a kind of trigger for powerful events. When you look back over your life, you will notice that situations tend to last for two-and-a-half year durations, while phases of five, seven-and-a-half or ten years are often also important.

Where to Start

Start by looking at the sign that the Moon is in, then look at the house and finally, check out the decan. Don't rush: take your time.

The Moon through Aries or the First House

This is a time of rebirth. You will be forced to abandon old ways of life and to look around for something new. You will feel more passionate about everything, and even if you are normally placid, you will be more enthusiastic and excited about life. The ego comes to the fore and you begin to demand more out of life for yourself. This can lead to conflicts with others, especially with other family members, authority figures and those who seek to restrict you. The emotions rise to the surface, making you more susceptible to love and passion and also to moody feelings and a general dissatisfaction with your past way of life. Your rather raw and tender feelings will be a contributory factor in family arguments. You may have to deal with females in the family in quite a serious manner.

Familiar patterns of life begin to break up. In working life, there will be new contacts, new ideas and many short-term schemes. New ways of working can occur at this time. Travel or connections with the sea are possible now. You will be more self-centred and more inclined to look after your own needs, rather than those of others. Your sex drive will increase and this may also contribute to a change of partnerships. Even if you don't change partners, a move of house and new family groupings and arrangements are likely to happen around you. You will be less able to put up with the limits that your previous lifestyle has set upon you.

16: THE MOON THROUGH THE SIGNS & HOUSES

The Moon through Taurus or the Second House
This is the start of a more settled and comfortable phase in which you put projects that you started earlier into steady action. Material matters become important now and you will make a start on getting a nice home together or buying land that you can grow things on. You will begin to make and keep money at this time, and any goods that you buy will be durable. You will become reluctant to lend or waste money, while speculative ventures will hold no interest for you.

Anything that you start to do now is meant to last. This is a good time to form business partnerships, especially with women, and these too will last. Emotional partnerships should also be much more durable, but they lack intensity and passion and you will be happier to found a stable family than to flit from lover to lover. You will become keen on art, music, dancing, photography and anything else that has a connection to form and beauty. Building, gardening, cooking, decorating your home and other such creative interests will hold your interest.

The Moon through Gemini or the Third House
You will be more restless than before and you will probably pack as much as you can into your life just to keep yourself from becoming bored. This is a time for mental exploration and you will have an urge to educate yourself. You would be particularly keen to communicate with others and you may begin to use these skills in a job of work. This could lead you into office work, sales, teaching and other forms of communication. Temporary work, short-term jobs or peripatetic may suit you.

Local issues will become part of your life, and you could get together with friends and neighbours in order to improve your area or raise funds for a local school. You can expect plenty of visits to places of local interest and also plenty of people coming to visit you at your home. Love and romance may be put on the back burner for the time being, because you will be more interested in improving your mental processes rather than your love life. However, connections with intelligent and interesting people could enhance your personal life. You may flirt more and be less inclined to stick faithfully to the same old partner. Your emotions may confuse you because they will get in the way of logic and clarity of perception.

The Moon through Cancer or the Fourth House

The Moon is comfortable in this sign or house but that doesn't necessarily mean that your life is guaranteed to be happy throughout the whole progression, because you may become moody and prone to greater emotional highs and lows and it may be hard for you to understand your own feelings at times. The past will draw your attention and you may take an interest in history or in collecting things that have a history attached to them. You may bore your family and friends by frequently referring to things that happened in the past.

Family life comes to the fore under this progression and you may set up a home and a family. A change of address is possible or perhaps the acquisition of a shop or some other kind of premises. You may become attached to someone else's home for a while. Feelings of family loyalty become stronger and you may fancy researching your family tree. The need to identify with a particular group, race or religion will exert a powerful tug. You may retreat from the world and immerse yourself in domesticity or alternatively, you could begin to run a small business from your home.

Your intuitive and psychic abilities will come to the fore. Your emotions will bring periods of jealousy, possessiveness and loneliness, even when these emotions are unfounded. You may want to be alone and yet fear being lonely. In a lighter vein, you will seek out novelties by visiting new places, especially those with a history to them, and travel will become more important to you.

The Moon through Leo or the Fifth House

This progression should bring you into contact with babies, children or young people. There could be babies born into your circle or you may take up a job or hobby in connection with children or young children. Your own behaviour will become more playful and childlike and you will begin to look around for pastimes and hobbies that allow you to play.

Creativity is the watchword now and this need will energise you into creating something important. You may write the definitive novel or creative a painting to rival that of the great masters, but it could just as easily be the creation of a home, a business, a family or a worthy cause that occupies your attention. Creative hobbies will appeal to you now because a creative outlet will be a necessity. You also need the attention that creative success will bring you. You will become bored with mundane jobs and begin to seek a job with a touch of glamour about it.

Your optimistic attitude could lead you to open your own business. You need to be somebody that people notice and your light cannot now be hidden under a bushel. Your feelings will rise to the surface and they may be hard to control. If you have spend your life thus far being kept down, your oppressors are in for a surprise or two. Exciting love affairs may become a feature of your life now, especially if you have been putting up with a dull or meaningless partnership. You will need an outlet for your passions.

The Moon through Virgo or the Sixth House
This is a great time to take up a new career because all forms of work will prosper now. This is especially so if the job is analytical in nature or if it concerns communications or the medical field. Bookkeeping, record keeping and office equipment could become an important feature of your life now. Do-it-yourself work, dressmaking or any other creative craft that requires dexterity and concentration would succeed at this time, as would writing or acting. You may take up farming or gardening.

This is a good time to establish sensible work habits and also to take on staff to help you cope. You may take up some form of training in order to brush up your skills and, even if you don't, you are sure to learn much that will be useful to you in the future. Your mind will become sharper and so will your sense of humour. You may become interested in health and healing, either of the normal medical variety or in the alternative therapy field. There may be an attachment to clinics, hospitals or doctor's surgeries due to family health problems or to finding a job in such a place. You will have to avoid taking on too much and working so hard that your nerves become stretched.

You may become faddy about food. Guilty feelings may plague you and you could become far too critical of yourself and others. Working relationships are more likely to be formed than personal ones. One rather nice compensatory factor for this all-work-and-no play syndrome is that it is a favourable time to buy new clothes.

The Moon through Libra or the Seventh House
Partnerships and relationships are the most significant feature of this progression and you will split away from some of those who have been a feature of your life and then form new partnerships. Your emotions will be strong and they may be at odds with your needs, possibly because you want security and freedom at the same time. This progression is best used for exploring new relationships than for outright commitment,

except in the business sphere when it works very well. This is an excellent time for all forms of business; especially where you have to act as an agent or assure that fair play is the rule. You will take care of your appearance and generally behave in an attractive and pleasant manner both at work and in your personal life. Legal matters may need to be attended to at this time, especially partnership agreements.

The Moon through Scorpio or the Eighth House
This progression brings crucial events because it is associated with the most vital aspects of life. There may be births and deaths in the family and among your friends. This is a time when one moves up a generation. Any form of separation, divorce and other losses will be compensated for by forming new relationships. Business relationships that tie you financially will be formed now and other people's financial situations will be important. There will be dealings with the legal and official aspects of money and business in the form of mortgages, taxation, legacies and corporate matters of all kinds. There may be legal wrangles over property or goods relating to partnerships that have ended.

You could up a new home or place of business with someone new and fortunately, there are great opportunities opening up for moneymaking. Investigations will become important, and these may take the form of medical investigations, police or other types of investigations. Psychic and mystical matters may interest to you and your level of intuition will increase. This is likely to be a very stressful time for both positive and negative reasons and you will end this period feeling wrung out but a new lifestyle will be the outcome. You should make some really good financial gains during this period.

The Moon through Sagittarius or the Ninth House
This progression will expand your horizons. You will be contact with foreigners, foreign goods and ideas that emerge from cultures and backgrounds that are different from yours. You may choose to live in another country for a while and also to learn another language and you could fall in love with a foreigner. This may lead you to investigate religions and philosophies that are different from yours. You may decide to take up some form of higher education, and the subject you choose could well have a philosophical aspect to it. You may be involved with schools, colleges and churches as part of your daily life or you could take courses.

Legal matters could become an important part of your life now. There should be a lot more fun in your life under this progression. You may take up hobbies and pastimes or become enthusiastic about sports. You may become more than usually interested in spiritual concepts such as mediumship, spiritual healing, reincarnation and astrology. Your values will become more spiritual and less materialistic and your sense of humour will become sharper. You will need to guard against over-optimism or expanding your horizons too quickly.

The Moon through Capricorn or the Tenth House
You will work hard while the Moon is in this sign or house and there will be a number of large and prestigious projects for you to complete. Details will need attention and you may feel at times as though you are being overwhelmed by work and responsibilities. You may suffer setbacks, and some sphere your life may become limited or restricted. A chronic ailment may surface and you could feel old and tired at times. Older people or those in positions of authority will do much to help you reach your goals and in the end, all the hard work will have been worth it. It will be easy for you to sell a product or a service at this time.

You will learn how to work in a structured and businesslike manner. Your work could bring you into contact with the public. You will take a sensitive attitude to colleagues and employees. Personal and business relationships will become blurred and you may begin to work with someone you love or fall in love with a person you meet through your work. This is not a truly romantic time, and your feelings may need to be kept under a tight control. It may not be possible to be with the one you love as much as you would like.

Domestic life will take a back seat while you concentrate on your career. Parents, older people and authority figures will become an important feature of your life now. You could become a grandparent yourself under this progression. Your attitude will be quite materialistic at this time, and you must guard against becoming hard and calculating, or working yourself into the ground.

The Moon through Aquarius or the Eleventh House
Friends will become an important feature of your life at this time and you will have more dealings with other people than formerly. You will feel the need to be identified with a particular group of people who share your views and represent a lifestyle that you aspire to. There

may be a cause or a movement that attracts you now. At work, you will have to work as part of a team or in charge of a group, and you will not be able to achieve too much on your own. You will strive for independence and you could seek to leave a situation that no longer works for you. There will be contact with helpful women but there could also be differences of opinion.

The urge to learn new things will lead you to seek education or to gain new skills. Modern methods and equipment will begin to fascinate you now. You will redefine your hopes and wishes and you may seek a completely different direction to the one you have followed up to now. Guard against becoming destructive, irrational or eccentric, and try not to push those who love you away. The chances are that the situation that you are in at the start of the progression will change radically by the time you end it. During this two-and-a-half year period, you could change your job, partner, home, family or even your country.

The Moon through Pisces or the Twelfth House
This will be a time of reflection and retreat and you may feel like a hermit at times, either staying quietly at home, working from home or not feeling sociable. You will become kinder and nicer but also more vulnerable, and your own personality may have to be suppressed for the sake of others or for the common good.

You will become involved with secrets, possibly due to starting something but not being able to talk openly about it for a while. There could be any amount of secret romantic entanglements, or you may be wrongly accused. Your family may find an excuse to exclude you from the fold. You must strive to keep hold of reality now, and not find yourself falling into a strange emotional morass, so try to avoid drink, drugs and opiates if you can. You may work in a prison, hospital or some other secluded place. You may travel to the sea or even move near water.

Artistic and creative skills will develop and you could learn to become quite competent at something creative. Metaphysical and psychic concepts will begin to interest you and you could develop a real flair for something different. You will be notice a great increase in your intuitive perception and probably real flashes of ESP. You must try not to become the architect of your own undoing with this progression.

Chapter Seventeen:
Solar Aspects

It would be nice to look at every aspect in detail and then into all the possible events that could occur under each aspect, but in a book of this length, we can only take a generalised view. I suggest that you treat yourself to a few books on transits and use the data for every kind of progression as well. Offer to make up charts for your pals and predict events for them, because their feedback will be very informative.

Sun/Sun
Easy aspects
- A good time for self-expression.
- Health improves.
- Creativity comes to the fore.
- Children and young people will bring joy.
- Romance will be fun and leisure pursuits amusing.

Challenging aspects
- This could be a frustrating and lonely time when others seem to be against you rather than with you.
- You may become intolerant or you may draw intolerance to you.
- This is a bad time to seek favours, especially from those in positions of authority or responsibility, and it is unlikely that you will be able to influence anyone else either.
- Children could become a problem to you now, while children who undergo this aspect themselves will feel unloved and misunderstood.

Sun/Moon
Easy aspects
- An improvement in domestic circumstances ranging from moving house to refurbishing a home.
- Improved family relationships and harmony between the women of the family.

- Children do well and there could be something to celebrate on their behalf.
- You will contact old friends and could even look up an ex-lover.
- Romance will go well as would a holiday on or by water.
- Small business interests do well now, especially shops, farms and anything vaguely domestic.

Challenging aspects
- Family and home situations are likely to be difficult and older women in particular could be difficult.
- You may feel at odds with yourself and it will be hard to become "centred" at this time. Romantic situations could crumble.
- Arguments will arise over money and there could be some very different views of who should spend what and how in your household.
- Business matters may suffer, especially small businesses of your own.
- Creative ventures will be difficult.
- The best thing is to keep to a routine, avoid arguments and try to learn as much as you can from this experience.

Sun/Mercury

Easy aspects
- A great time to learn something new or teach something to others.
- Neighbours, colleagues and friends could figure strongly in your life now, as could brothers and sisters. All of these could come up with great ideas.
- A new vehicle is a possibility.
- You may take up an intelligent hobby or a creative venture. Negotiations will go well.

Challenging aspects
- Try not to allow pride or intolerance to spoil things for you.
- Watch what you say and how you say it, because your mouth may have a tendency to run away with itself.
- Avoid being malicious behind people's backs.
- Games and gambling are likely to go wrong and this is definitely not the time to take up competitive sports of any kind.

Sun/Venus

Easy aspects
- This brings a great improvement in your social life.

- Romance, friendship and everything associated with having a good time will be on the menu for you now.
- Art, music, dancing, leisure and pleasure will all play a part in your life at this time.
- You will use your charm to captivate others and your looks will improve dramatically now.
- If you have neglected your appearance or allowed your wardrobe to become jaded, this is the time to make changes.

Challenging aspects
- You may become lazy under this influence and put on weight.
- You aren't interested in exercise, self-control or dedication to hard work at this time.
- You may be tempted to spend money, either on your own behalf or on behalf of your children and you may not want to admit the nastier sides of their nature - or yours.
- Anything to do with art, beauty and creativity will be held up now and your social life will be very quiet.
- Family celebrations will cause hassle.
- Romance may go badly, but your sex life could take off.

Sun/Mars
Easy aspects
- These two fiery and energetic planets can combine to give you a great time.
- Your courage will be at its peak and you will feel that you can take on the world.
- This is a great time to get involved in anything competitive.
- If you decide to do anything really dangerous, do make sure that you take extra care because cutting corners could cost you your life.
- Men of influence may enter your life now and your own status and financial standing could increase now.
- You may take up something glamourous or you may simply appear more glamourous than ever before to those who count.
- You may make love more frequently and more passionately than usual.

Challenging aspects
- You could suddenly become quite aggressive, impulsive, argumentative and difficult.

- ~ A competitive streak could suddenly emerge and you may become keen on dangerous sports.
- ~ You will have to guard against accidents associated with weapons or machinery.
- ~ Impulsive financial speculation can lead to losses, and uncontrolled desires can lead to almost anything!
- ~ Keep control of your temper and of your life.

Sun/Jupiter

Easy aspects
- ~ This is a great time to learn something new and to explore new ideas of all kinds.
- ~ You may take a course of training at this time.
- ~ If you fall in love now, it will be by finding someone who feels the same way as you do and who shares your beliefs.
- ~ You will take charge of your life and you may have considerable responsibility and leadership thrust upon you.
- ~ Political aims, recognition and support are on the way to you now.
- ~ You could travel now or become involved with foreigners, foreign goods or foreign organisations.
- ~ Legal matters would also go well.

Challenging aspects
- ~ This can lead to arrogance, intolerance and an exaggerated idea of your own importance. There may be too much expansion in some area of your life and you could go totally over the top in anything from a philosophical belief to a business venture.
- ~ Your attitude will be impractical and this will create problems in all your relationships with others.
- ~ You may become extravagant or there may be unavoidable losses.
- ~ Foreigners and foreign travel may prove difficult, as could legal or educational matters.

Sun/Saturn

Easy aspects
- ~ Hard work that has been done in the past will bring rewards now.
- ~ Older people will be cooperative and those in positions of responsibility or authority will be approachable and helpful.

17: SOLAR ASPECTS

- ~ You may have some extra responsibility thrust upon you now but you won't be unbeneficial about this.
- ~ Sensible people will enter your life and any relationship that has been unsettled will steady itself down into a workable pattern.
- ~ Your mood will be rather serious and any groups or organisations that you associate with now will also have a rather serious outlook and purpose to them.

Challenging aspects
- ~ Personal ambition and creativity will be stifled for a while and everything will be hard to achieve.
- ~ Social life and romance will probably disappear, and illness or depression could limit your activities for a while.
- ~ You may become cold, hard and rigid in your opinions and you may try to use your position and status in order to push others around.
- ~ You will find it hard to gain recognition and even harder to find love.
- ~ Children may be a burden to you at this time and, children themselves who are under this progression will feel unloved.

Sun/Uranus
Easy aspects
- ~ You will feel an urge to break out of your usual mould and seek the freedom to be yourself and to do your own thing.
- ~ You will wish to develop your creative ideas in many new and original directions.
- ~ Friends and like-minded groups will appeal strongly to you and these could have a strong influence on you now.
- ~ You will wish to look inside yourself and to achieve your own personal goals.
- ~ You may become involved with politics or causes of some kind.
- ~ Novel subjects may begin to appeal to you or you could become interested in science, engineering, information technology or something similar.
- ~ You could fall head over heels with someone to whom you feel a magnetic attraction but it may not last.

Challenging aspects
- ~ Your behaviour could become completely incomprehensible under this transit and you may vacillate between one kind of belief and another.
- ~ Nobody will be able to work out what you are going to do next.

- You will find life unpredictable and unsettled for a while and you may end the transit or progression by changing your way of life forever.
- Restlessness and eccentricity will drive you to break out of your rut and make changes.
- There will be changes in connection with friends and also with children at this time.
- You may leave a group of people who you have been associated with for some time past or you may decide to join a new and different group of people now.

Sun/Neptune
Easy aspects
- Your creative instincts will come to the fore at this time and you may wish to lend your support to people or organisations in the creative field.
- You could deal successfully with hospitals, institutions and homes for the elderly now.
- There will be an increased interest in religion, philosophy, spiritualism or even astrology, and you may seek to instruct children in these subjects.
- Art and music will appeal to you.
- You may wish to delve into your past and discover the patterns that have shaped your life.
- Many people experience an increase in psychic experiences at this time, especially precognitive dreams.

Challenging aspects
- It will be hard to keep a grip on your life now and you must take care who you trust.
- Partnerships may be extremely strange or ultimately disappointing.
- You must take care in business, romance and just about everything else that is important in life.
- You may overdo things in many ways, either by falling in love with the wrong person or by taking a real interest in drink or drug abuse.
- Delusions of grandeur or any other kind of delusion could make you hard to fathom.
- You may become quite psychic, especially in connection with dreams.
- Avoid medical treatments at this time if you can and be very careful about any medication that you take.
- Children may drive you crazy at this time.

Sun/Pluto
Easy aspects
- ~ This marks an important time of transition in your life.
- ~ You may marry, divorce, take up a new career, retire, move to another country or do anything else that represents a major change of life.
- ~ Guard against illness at this time and, if you do get ill, then you will need to take this into account as part of the changing pattern of your life.
- ~ Business matters related to banks, tax, corporations, legacies and shared financial resources are likely to become important now.
- ~ You may have to change your personal financial status as a result of the actions of others. Shared resources, such as in marriage could become an issue.
- ~ You will want to look more deeply into the meaning of everything and some aspect of investigating will become part of your life.

Challenging aspects
- ~ You will have to take care in all business dealings and also in connection with taxes, legal matters, corporate matters and other people's money.
- ~ Guard against becoming involved in power struggles at work or in sexual relationships.
- ~ Sex, birth, death and the deeper aspects of life could cause you problems.
- ~ You will have to make some kind of transformation to your lifestyle but this may work out well in the end.

Sun/Chiron
Easy aspects
- ~ If you or anyone in your circle has been ill lately, this will improve.
- ~ You may become interested in alternative therapies and all other matters related to health. You could wish to help others by treating or counselling them.
- ~ Teaching and learning will become important to you, especially in connection with the development of children.
- ~ You may become interested in music or the martial arts, even something like Tai Chi.

Challenging aspects
- ~ Watch your health and also the health of those who are around you.
- ~ You may want to teach others how to live, only to find that they don't want to listen.
- ~ Relationships and work could cause problems for a while now.

Sun/the Nodes
Easy aspects
- This would be a good time to move house or to improve the one you have.
- Family matters will go well and anything that you try to achieve out in the world will succeed now too.
- The atmosphere around you will be conducive to success and the political "zeitgeist" will suit you. You may receive some kind of karmic benefit.

Challenging aspects
- It may be hard to get the world to accept your ideas.
- Family life will be difficult and anything domestic will be a bit awkward, too.
- There may be some kind of karmic debt to be paid.

Sun/Ascendant
Easy aspects
- This is a good time for a fresh start and to assert yourself.
- New friends, increased social life and a time of fun should be around you now.
- Health should improve with this aspect.

Challenging aspects
- There could be problems with children or with creative projects.
- Guard against becoming egotistical.

Sun/Midheaven
Easy aspects
- This is a great time to seek recognition, to forge ahead with career aims or simply to make up your mind as to what you want from life and then start to go out and get it.
- People in positions of authority should be helpful.
- Clean up your home, your office and your act now, you have everything to gain and nothing to lose.

Challenging aspects
- Problems associated with authority figures could feature now and your own authority will be challenged.
- It will be hard to achieve your objectives for a while.

Chapter Eighteen:
Lunar Aspects

When doing day-for-a-year progressions, these lunar aspects assume a terrific importance. When coupled with transits, this is probably the most accurate and interesting form of predictive astrology of all. Each progression will last for about a month, but it can have a tremendous impact on your life, with the effects lasting far beyond the month in question. Lunar aspects are the triggers of your life, setting off trains of events that are fascinating to watch and to live through.

Moon/Moon
Easy aspects
- ~ This would be a good time to change your address or to invest in property.
- ~ Family matters will go well as will anything that involves women or women's interests.
- ~ You may be emotional and rather restless at this time.
- ~ Travel is well aspected now.

Challenging aspects
- ~ Domestic and family matters are likely to be strained just now and this is a bad time to call in the builders or to try to move house.
- ~ Your emotions will be stretched and you may go down with some kind of ailment as a result of stress.
- ~ Travel is not well starred, although you are restless enough to try it anyway.

Moon/Mercury
Easy aspects
- ~ Your curiosity will be stimulated and the harnessing of your imagination to your intellect could have very interesting results.
- ~ Travel around your locality will be well starred now.
- ~ Business matters, especially those that require negotiation, trading or communication will go well now.

- This is a good time to enjoy sporting activities, and also the company of younger people.
- You will enjoy the company of brothers and sisters.

Challenging aspects
- The car may let you down, your local buses and trains may go on strike or your bike will spring a puncture.
- Your temper will not be at its best.
- Domestic matters will become screwed up and some piece of machinery that you depend upon may suddenly develop a bad case of the gremlins.
- Older women will get you down and business matters will be delayed or difficult.
- Your brothers or sisters could aggravate you.

Moon/Venus

Easy aspects
- This is a wonderful time to fall in love!
- Be careful, because your feelings are vulnerable and close to the surface.
- There may be family celebrations and happy events of all kinds, especially those that bring you into contact with others in a social setting.
- Holidays, dinners and other outings will please you.
- You may become involved in something to do with music, beauty or other pleasant subjects.
- The money situation should improve but you may also be in a mood to spend money and if so, you will buy goods that are attractive, lasting and a little luxurious.

Challenging aspects
- Partnerships will be difficult and a romance may suddenly go wrong.
- You may fall in love with someone totally unsuitable because your feelings are vulnerable and you may not be able to think straight.
- Family celebrations and events will be a source of irritation and anything to do with domestic life will be fraught.
- Don't buy anything important now if you can help it, especially if it is something for the home.
- Women will be a source of aggravation; your health may not be the best.
- There may be more work than play for a while.
- Try not to become involved in any business dealings or money transactions now.

18: Lunar Aspects

Moon/Mars
Easy aspects
- ~ This aspect will heighten your feelings and it may make you rash or impetuous.
- ~ You will find it hard to keep your temper and you may fly off the handle all to easily.
- ~ It would be best to take your time now over any important decisions.
- ~ Dealings with men will be very interesting and this can mark the start of an important love affair.
- ~ Family and domestic matters should go well but your impatient attitude may make you irritable towards those who are close to you.

Challenging aspects
- ~ You may lose your temper.
- ~ Guard against accidents through rashness.
- ~ Family matters will be extremely irritating.
- ~ There may be health problems, even an operation or dental treatment.

Moon/Jupiter
Easy aspects
- ~ This is a good aspect if you want to deal with property or premises, and a move or refurbishment would work well.
- ~ Legal matters related to property or the family would also succeed.
- ~ You may become involved in religious or spiritual matters, possibly through coming into contact with interesting new people who introduce you to new concepts.
- ~ This is a good time to learn or to teach and if you need to take an examination, you should be successful in your endeavours.
- ~ Finances should pick up and there should be some excellent business opportunities with such matters as publishing or broadcasting being especially successful.
- ~ Foreigners, foreign travel or anything to do with foreign goods are all well starred.
- ~ Most of your schemes should succeed at this lucky time.
- ~ This can bring losses in one area whilst bringing gains in another.

Challenging aspects
- ~ This could be an expensive time with unexpected bills and few opportunities of finding any extra cash.
- ~ Dealings with property or legal matters will be difficult to manage.

- Any business that involves farming, food, women's issues, publishing, broadcasting or the general public will be awkward.
- You may find that your beliefs are being challenged and you may temporarily lose faith in your guardian angels or in yourself.
- Educational matters will go slowly.
- This is a poor time to travel or to deal with foreigners.

Moon/Saturn
Easy aspects
- This will heap a certain amount of extra responsibility on to your shoulders and it may be a time of very hard work.
- You could be a bit off colour at this time or just tired and feeling that you are being overworked and underpaid.
- You will finish all that you start now and you will be well rewarded for anything that you do.
- This is an excellent time in which to deal with those in authority over you and also to sort out anything regarding older relatives.
- Your own authority and status should improve.
- You must pay some extra attention to the home and to your family at this time and you will also take a serious attitude to domestic problems.
- Your emotions will be under control and you shouldn't be swept away by your feelings.

Challenging aspects
- A time of hard unremitting work and the rewards may not be obvious or quick to materialise.
- A chronic illness could suddenly assert itself.
- People in positions of authority could be very hard on you and life in general is likely to be unfair and difficult for a while.
- Parents and older relatives will be demanding and family life may be depressing.
- You may long to move house or to do something about your surroundings but you could be short of the time, money or the opportunity to do so.

Moon/Uranus
Easy aspects
- Uranus always brings the unexpected, but at least the surprises should be pleasant ones.

18: Lunar Aspects

- This should bring good news in connection with family and domestic matters and it could bring unexpected visitors or an opportunity to visit other people in their homes.
- You will make new friends and you could also join a group or an organisation that looks like being fun.
- Any business that concerns food, women's interests or domestic matters will go well.
- You may be a bit over emotional and over excited at times.

Challenging aspects
- There could be sudden events in connection with your home and family or among your friends.
- If you have been involved in a group activity for some time, there will be sudden changes.
- Nothing is certain now and your own mood is strangely rebellious, eccentric and awkward.
- You may want to make a bid for freedom and to cut all those ties that have become just a little too comfortable, familiar and boring.
- If other heavy aspects are involved, you will change your way of life quite dramatically.

Moon/Neptune
Easy aspects
- You will become a really sensitive soul.
- Neptune will make you compassionate towards the sufferings of others.
- Artistic and creative endeavours will do well; you could become keen on photography, poetry, music or anything else that evokes memories and feelings.
- You may find yourself looking back over your past and even reliving something that happened to you years ago.
- You will become more receptive to your inner feelings and you will notice an increase in your intuitive powers.
- Precognitive dreams are possible at this time.
- Daydreams are also possible and you may lose yourself in a time of dreaming and drifting for a while.

Challenging aspects
- You may feel as though your life is on a kind roller coaster with the chief victim being your own emotions.

- The past could come back to haunt you in some way and you may have to face up to some pretty awful memories or feelings that have been buried away for years.
- You will become over sensitive and terribly vulnerable.
- Guard against deception in financial and business dealings and if possible, leave any important decisions until well after this progression has passed.
- Artistic and creative ventures will be especially badly affected.

Moon/Pluto
Easy aspects
- You may decide to change your domestic circumstances, or even to move house.
- If this occurs when other important progressions or transits happen, it could be life changing.
- Important matters relating to births, deaths, beginnings and endings can go your way now and if you have to deal with legacies, taxes and other joint matters these should prosper now.
- Family matters are important at this time.
- There may be something good or difficult in the offing, relating to mothers or motherhood.
- Your sex life may suddenly pick up and both secret and open liaisons are likely to move into a more passionate phase now.

Challenging aspects
- You may find yourself facing up to something that in your heart of hearts, you have known was wrong for a long time.
- You may bring an affair of the heart to an end or make a start on a new one but whichever way this goes, there will be pain and soul-searching on a deep inner level.
- You may suddenly become frightened by psychic experiences or by people who are sinister.
- Don't become involved in business matters or partnership matters that involve shared resources.
- Legal and official matters can bring problems at this time and there could be family wrangles over wills, tax bills and so on.
- This is a poor time to buy property or to have major work done at home.
- Family life is likely to be a bit tense.

- Your sex life could become an issue and this too could lead you to take some difficult decisions.
- Dealings with births, deaths, beginnings and endings may bring problems.
- Old resentments may resurface.

Moon/Chiron
Easy aspects
- If you or anybody close to you has been ill lately, this should begin to improve rapidly.
- Your compassion for those who need help will be stimulated at this time.
- There could be some kind of strangely karmic or emotionally important event in your life, and you could learn a lot from this.

Challenging aspects
- This could bring health problems for you or your loved ones.
- If you work in the health or healing field, things may be tough for a while.
- Teaching or learning may present difficulties

Moon/the Nodes
Easy aspects
- This is likely to bring joy and happiness to your home.
- Business matters may go well and there may be a karmic feeling to everything that is going on.
- If you deal with the public, it will be a success.

Challenging aspects
- Your mother or other older relatives could be very demanding now and your mood is not a happy one.
- Home, household or domestic matters go badly.
- There may be some kind of karmic debt to be paid now.

Moon/Ascendant
Easy aspects
- Happy family life and a good mood all around you typify this event.
- You will feel optimistic and outgoing and anything that you start now should go well in the future.
- Domestic and family matters are well starred as are any business matters relating to farming, food, women's interests or the general public.

Challenging aspects
- Logic and intuition will be at odds with each other.

- You won't relate well to others and you may not understand yourself either for a while.
- This is not a great time for business, domestic life or matters of the heart.

Moon/Midheaven
Easy aspects
- If you need to improve your public image out in the world, this is the time to do it.
- Public relations and sales or marketing of any kind will succeed, as will domestic and family matters.
- This would be a good time to entertain important people at your place of work or in your home.

Challenging aspects
- This aspect will bring difficulties with your aims and ambitions.
- Business matters will not go well and there could be a conflict between your work and your home, with plenty of pressure coming at you from both sides.
- Your parents may not approve of what you are trying to do.
- This is a difficult time for real estate transactions or for working in anything that is supplied to women or which deals with the public.

Chapter Nineteen:
Planetary Aspects

Mercury/Mercury
Easy aspects
- ~ It's easy to learn something new or to teach others now.
- ~ Your curiosity will be stimulated and you will need to stretch your mind.
- ~ Relationships with neighbours, colleagues, brothers and sisters will be good and any local or family events will go well.
- ~ You may feel like becoming a writer or journalist or taking up a job that involves sales, communication of any kind or driving.

Challenging aspects
- ~ Your mind may become temporarily blocked but this will simply lead you into other ways of thinking.

Mercury/Venus
Easy aspects
- ~ This is great for business, romance or social life.
- ~ Negotiations and anything else to do with finances will succeed, as will any dealings with women.
- ~ You will want to spend money on your appearance and this will pay off both in personal and professional life.
- ~ You could become interested in art, beauty or music and anything to do with the preparation and enjoyment of good food is well starred.

Challenging aspects
- ~ Misunderstandings with siblings, neighbours and even those you love could occur.
- ~ You will find it hard to express yourself clearly, especially to those whom you love.
- ~ This is the wrong time to ask for a raise or to spend much money.

Mercury/Mars
Easy aspects
- An intense period of work.
- Good business ideas.
- You will think and act very quickly and can put this to good use in a business context.
- This should be a good time to sign papers and to work in partnership with men.
- Attraction to a person who shares your sporting and spare time interests is possible.
- Anger and aggression can be diverted into action but you may become somewhat sarcastic and cutting.
- Confidence increases.

Challenging aspects
- A bad time to be involved in any kind of business with others, or to sign important papers.
- There will be disagreements over work methods and new technology may be hard to get to grips with.
- Anger, biting sarcasm and bitter arguments are possible.
- A possible split from a man in business or personal life.

Mercury/Jupiter
Easy aspects
- This will be an educational phase in which you seek information and ideas on a big scale.
- Philosophy, religion and psychic matters will be put under the microscope and ministers of religion could enter your life.
- You may decide to expand business enterprises and the chances of negotiating good terms are excellent.
- New people in your life will open your eyes to great possibilities and travel of all kinds will be favourable.
- Legal matters will be successful.
- This is a great time to study, write or teach and foreigners could be a source of inspiration.

Challenging aspects
- You become muddled and confused about your beliefs.
- Conflicting ideas could confuse you.

- This is a bad time to become involved in legal matters or to agree to anything big that involves business negotiations.
- Don't sign anything important.
- Travel may be difficult. Foreigners or foreign goods could cause problems.

Mercury/Saturn
Easy aspects
- This is a good time to get your head down and concentrate on a course of study or on new work practices.
- Anything that is started now should be finished properly in due course.
- Nothing will happen quickly but progresses will be made.
- A realistic and methodical approach will pay off and there may be an interest in scientific or detailed work of some kind.
- Older people may be influential in business matters and an older relative could help you out.
- Family matters will be sorted out and there could be some travel to and from family members or on business.

Challenging aspects
- You may feel tongue tied and stupid at this time but if you can find a way of expressing yourself, you can succeed.
- Guard against losing your confidence.
- Hard work, especially in a scientific field can bring results and writing may be especially successful.
- Guard against problems due to sloppy financial or business practices.
- Avoid overwork or allowing a health problem to get out of hand.

Mercury/Uranus
Easy aspects
- This will stimulate your mind and take you into new realms of thought.
- Original and unusual ideas can be successfully pursued.
- You should make new friends and become involved in institutions, groups and social clubs that are stimulating and amusing.
- You may get new job or discover a new way of doing a current one.
- You may become involved in alternative therapies and spiritual healing and your intuition level will increase dramatically.

Challenging aspects
- Reliable machinery will be taken over by gremlins.
- You may have some very original ideas, but they may be too unrealistic.

- Your temper and your mental processes will be erratic and uncertain.
- There may be arguments with neighbours and siblings.
- Take care while driving or travelling around your locality for some time now.

Mercury/Neptune
Easy aspects
- You could fall in love with a dream that does not match up to reality.
- If it isn't love that fascinates you, the spiritual side of life will appeal.
- You will find it easier to visualise and to conceptualise at this time.
- Dreams may become reality now, and travel near or over water will be beneficial.
- This is a great time to put creative ideas into action and hobbies such as acting could prove to be fun.

Challenging aspects
- If you fall in love with a dream or a vision now, you could be in for a rude awakening later on!
- Guard against becoming involved with deceitful people, losers, betrayers or those who seek to destroy your confidence.
- Drinkers and druggies may be tremendously appealing but they are all part of the illusion.
- There may be scandal, loss and difficulties in dealing with people in business or legal matters.
- Try not to travel or become involved with foreigners for the time being if you can avoid it.
- Psychic or psychological problems may arise.

Mercury/Pluto
Easy aspects
- There will be an increased interest in shared resources or merging with others in any way.
- You will want to look behind and beneath every question and it will be easy for you to solve mysteries now.
- This would be a great time to write a successful thriller!
- You may take an interest in psychic matters and you will want to know how these work.
- You will want to improve your education and probably your financial position as well.
- You will be able to communicate with others on many levels.

- There could be legal dealings, possibly as a result of deaths in the family and siblings may well be involved in these matters.
- You will want to look into matters relating to birth, death and sex!

Challenging aspects
- Business could go wrong, and legal matters could become a minefield.
- You may even have to pay someone to investigate a particular problem or a situation.
- This is not a good time to sign anything important, and you should take care over matters relating to taxes, mortgages and so on.
- Avoid becoming involved in strange psychic experiences or practices.
- There may be difficulties in connection with siblings and neighbours.
- Sex may bring problems.

Mercury/Chiron
Easy aspects
- Study, teach and take up any interest in health or healing.
- Sporting interests are favourable.
- If you or anyone in your family have been ill lately, they will soon recover.

Challenging aspects
- Health is the big problem here and any ailment that occurs now could hang around for long time.
- Studying, teaching and sporting interests would be problematical.
- Take care of any sick people who are around you.

Mercury/the Nodes
Easy aspects
- Depending upon the node that is involved, past experiences or completely new ideas could be very successful.
- Anything that you do now will fit well with the public mood, and any form of public relations or image polishing would be a great success.
- Property and family dealings will succeed.

Challenging aspects
- Property matters will bring problems and family life is not easy now.
- Don't take chances in business now.

Mercury/Ascendant
Easy aspects
- ~ Your confidence is on the increase and your sense of initiative and enterprise is building all the time.
- ~ Your communications ability will be on the increase and all business matters should go well.

Challenging aspects
- ~ Guard against over-expansion in business and watch what you agree to.
- ~ Think before you speak and don't allow others to sap your confidence.

Mercury/Midheaven
Easy aspects
- ~ A great time for business enterprises or for forging ahead in any sphere of life that requires communication ability.
- ~ A career change or a change of your direction is quite likely.
- ~ If you deserve a raise or a promotion, ask for it now.

Challenging aspects
- ~ Difficulties connected with your aims and ambitions are likely to arise.

Venus/Venus
Easy aspects
- ~ You will appreciate music, art and beauty in all its forms.
- ~ Women could be very helpful to you, and life should be pleasant and easy.
- ~ It will be easy to make money and very pleasant to spend it.
- ~ People in your circle will be friendly, helpful and sociable and you will be able to impress them with your charm and charisma.
- ~ You may fall in love.

Challenging aspects
- ~ Difficulties in connection with money or relationships.
- ~ Women may pose problems.
- ~ You may be unhappy with your looks or your image.

Venus/Mars
Easy aspects
- ~ A love affair could be on the cards.
- ~ A time to spend money on luxuries.
- ~ You might take an active interest in artistic or creative pursuits.

Challenging aspects
- ~ Guard against allowing your feelings to run away with you.
- ~ Don't allow greedy people to use you as a meal ticket.

Venus/Jupiter
Easy aspects
- ~ You can afford to take a gamble.
- ~ You should be able to enjoy whatever you are doing.
- ~ The culture and beliefs of those you come into contact with will influence you beneficially.
- ~ There may be travel in connection with business.

Challenging aspects
- ~ Over expansion could lead to losses.
- ~ Travel may be expensive.

Venus/Saturn
Easy aspects
- ~ Creative ventures may be slow going but, once the work has been put into them, they should be successful.
- ~ Friendships and acquaintanceships will be rather pleasant and relationships with older relatives will also be nice.
- ~ This is, indeed, a very difficult time for love relationships, because on the one hand, they could become durable at present, but on the other hand, they may well bring trials and tribulations to follow in their wake.

Challenging aspects
- ~ This could mark a difficult time for all relationships.
- ~ Money will be hard to come by and you may feel off colour as well.

Venus/Uranus
Easy aspects
- ~ Sudden attractions are possible.
- ~ New friendships and exciting people and experiences are likely now and live will be pleasantly unpredictable.
- ~ Work that involves electronics could prove to be viable.

Challenging aspects
- ~ You may fall for the wrong person.
- ~ You may take a job, only to find it doesn't work for you.

- You get into the wrong crowd.
- You may be eased out of a position in a group or an organisation.

Venus/Neptune
Easy aspects
- This is a really dreamy and romantic phase.
- You may put your lover on a pedestal and not be able to see reality for the mists of romance.
- This is a good time to be compassionate and charming towards others.

Challenging aspects
- Romance could go wrong and losses can occur in business.
- Avoid drugs, sex and rock and roll if you can.

Venus/Pluto
Easy aspects
- Powerful feelings will become apparent and you could even find yourself falling in love.
- You benefit from a legacy, pension or tax rebate.

Challenging aspects
- Watch your heart and your bank account!

Venus/Chiron
Easy aspects
- You should be healthy, and sick relatives or friends will begin to recover.
- A woman may teach you something useful.

Challenging aspects
- Chiron aspects can be difficult for health and relationships.

Venus/the Nodes
Easy aspects
- A good time to spend money on property.
- A good time for business dealings that benefit the public.
- You may meet a soul mate.

Challenging aspects
- You may be drawn to something or someone who is wrong for you.

Venus/Ascendant
Easy aspects
- ~ Make a start on improving your image, your appearance and your finances.
- ~ You will become happier and easier to get along with.
- ~ You may look for someone to love, or get involved in something creative.

Challenging aspects
- ~ Relationship difficulties and a loss of inspiration.

Venus/Midheaven
Easy aspects
- ~ A great time to forge ahead with your aims, ambitions or making money.
- ~ Romance could lead to business opportunities or you could meet someone through work.
- ~ You will look good and feel good about yourself.
- ~ Good relationships with parents, in-laws, bosses and older people.

Challenging aspects
- ~ Life becomes a bit of grind and rather boring for a while.

Mars/Mars
Easy aspects
- ~ A very busy phase in which you can get a great deal done.
- ~ Your energy level will be high and you will make decisions quickly.
- ~ Jobs that are traditionally considered to be masculine, such as engineering, car maintenance and building may become part of your life now.

Challenging aspects
- ~ Guard against rashness, accidents and hastily handling sharp objects.
- ~ Take care while driving.

Mars/Jupiter
Easy aspects
- ~ This brings an expansion in business or cultural affairs.
- ~ Business travel, or exploring new faces and places is indicated.
- ~ Groups or organisations that are involved in religion, astrology or spiritual matters might appeal to you.

Challenging aspects
- ~ Beware of over expansion in any area of your life, and take care while travelling.
- ~ Avoid dealing with aggressive men and overtly dangerous situations.

Mars/Saturn
Easy aspects
- ~ You can forge ahead very successfully now.
- ~ Progress in career matters and an increase in status are possible.
- ~ Older people, those in authority or men in general may help you.
- ~ You may find yourself dealing in a beneficial way with people who wear uniforms or who work in the fields of engineering or science.

Challenging aspects
- ~ You may find it hard to achieve your ambitions and there may be people who try to stand in your way.
- ~ You may become resentful and angry and lose your temper as a result.

Mars/Uranus
Easy aspects
- ~ Your emotions may be hard to control and a hectic love affair is possible.
- ~ You should put your heart into new and original ideas.
- ~ You could take up a sport, a course of education or training.
- ~ Your confidence level should increase.

Challenging aspects
- ~ Guard against accidents or losses through hasty behaviour.
- ~ Arguments are likely.

Mars/Neptune
Easy aspects
- ~ Your psychic powers and intuition will be on the increase and you could meet people who inspire you to take an interest in spiritual matters.
- ~ If you are interested in any kind of creative endeavour, this will begin to go very well.
- ~ Behind the scenes work or any selfless help that you give to others will be worthwhile.

Challenging aspects
- ~ You could fall in love, become obsessed and get hurt as a result.
- ~ Your sexual drive is very high and it could lead you into trouble.
- ~ Avoid drink, drugs and the lower levels of life.

Mars/Pluto
Easy aspects
- ~ You will want to push things to the limit and your increased will power will enable you to do so.
- ~ You may reach a position of influence or power.
- ~ This is an excellent time to deal with business matters, especially those that involve joint finances.
- ~ Sexual and relationship matters could be spectacular.

Challenging aspects
- ~ Power struggles and temper tantrums are possible.
- ~ Try to avoid political situations or places that could put you in a dangerous position.
- ~ Business matters and relationships with others could be frustrating due to power struggles. Sex could be a problem, or it could cause one.

Mars/Chiron
Easy aspects
- ~ You may want to heal the sick, or learn some form of medicine or healing.
- ~ You may study or teach some kind of sports.
- ~ You may find a mentor for your more spiritual interests.

Challenging aspects
- ~ Guard against accidents and look after yourself.
- ~ Take care of your knees, shins, calves, ankles and feet.
- ~ Avoid dealing with weapons of any kind.

Mars/the Nodes
Easy aspects
- ~ This is a good time for property dealings.
- ~ You may get together with family members and either plan for the future or reminisce about the past.
- ~ Anything that you take up now will be well received by the public.
- ~ There may be a karmic benefit from good that you have done in the past.
- ~ Life is easy for a change.

Challenging aspects
- ~ Family and domestic difficulties.
- ~ A feeling that you are swimming against the tide.

Mars/Ascendant
Easy aspects
- ~ A time to break out of your rut and make a fresh start.
- ~ You will be more self-centred than usual, but this is probably a good thing.

Challenging aspects
- ~ It is hard to get anything off the ground now.
- ~ You may be feeling off colour.
- ~ People could be awkward and obstreperous.

Mars/Midheaven
Easy aspects
- ~ This is a good time to put all your energies into getting on and making achievements.
- ~ A man may help you reach your goals.
- ~ Try to rest if you can because the chances are that you are working very hard at this time.
- ~ If you want a raise or a promotion, ask for it now.

Challenging aspects
- ~ Someone may stand in the way of your progress and there could be a series of frustrating arguments as a result.
- ~ This is not a good time to ask for a raise or for anything else that you deserve or want.

Chapter Twenty:
The Slower Moving Planets

Here I have only given the positive interpretation, but if the aspect is a negative one, just turn the positive on its head.

For instance, if Jupiter is square to Jupiter, expect a lack of new options, no opportunity to expand horizons and travel won't go well.

Jupiter/Jupiter
- ~ New opportunities, travel and expansion of horizons.
- ~ Legal matters go well as do educational and spiritual matters.

Jupiter/Saturn
- ~ Expand cautiously, especially in speculative ventures.
- ~ Older people or those who have a spiritual outlook may be helpful.

Jupiter/Uranus
- ~ A time of massive expansion.
- ~ Original and unusual people and ideas can lead you into new directions.
- ~ Unexpected luck.
- ~ A good time to deal with your local government.

Jupiter/Neptune
- ~ A great time for travel over or near water.
- ~ Expansion of ideas, especially spiritual and mystical ones will be interesting and successful.
- ~ Healing and mediumship would be especially attractive at this time.
- ~ Money can be made from creative endeavours.

Jupiter/Pluto
- ~ Spiritual matters will come to the fore now and you should experience an increase in your level of intuition.
- ~ You may develop an interest in health and healing or in legal matters.

Jupiter/the Nodes
- ~ Luck in connection with property, family life, work affecting the public.
- ~ Karmic benefits.

Jupiter/Ascendant
- ~ A fresh start with everything to play for.
- ~ Great expansion of horizons.

Jupiter/Midheaven
- ~ Could be a terrific time for all career matters, progress may be fast or slow but it is ensured.
- ~ You may find a spiritual belief that changes your life for the better.

Saturn/Saturn
- ~ A time of facing reality.
- ~ Your life may change for the better or the worse but there will be a period of hard work and of sorting yourself out on an inner level.

Saturn/Uranus
- ~ Uranus wants to forge ahead and Saturn puts on the brakes.
- ~ Others notice you, and you can achieve much in something political.
- ~ You will be able to put modern techniques to good use and a realistic attitude to original ideas can bring wonderful rewards.
- ~ You will take responsibility in some kind of group activity and friends will become an important part of your life.

Saturn/Neptune
- ~ You may work on a successful secret project.
- ~ You may tap into your spiritual or intuitive abilities in a useful manner.
- ~ Creative enterprises will be hard work but they can be brought to fruition
- ~ Love affairs can prosper under this progression or transit and they would combine common sense and idealistic romance.

Saturn/Pluto
- ~ Your concentration will increase.
- ~ You can make progress in a large project that involves large and important organisations.
- ~ Ambitions can be achieved.

20: The Slower Moving Planets

Saturn/Nodes
- ~ Steady progress at home.
- ~ The political or prevailing situation in your environment will help you to achieve your ambitions.
- ~ There may be some karmic benefit from the past or even from a past life.

Saturn/Ascendant
- ~ A time of progress if you work hard and concentrate on details.
- ~ You may become rather shy and withdrawn or so devoted to your ambitions that you ignore your loved ones.

Saturn/Midheaven
- ~ People in authority can help you now.
- ~ Forge ahead with your ambitions but avoid becoming cold and hard.

Uranus/Uranus
- ~ Take to break out from your mould.
- ~ Friends may exert a strong influence on your life now.
- ~ Original and unusual ideas will appeal to you and you may become unpredictable and eccentric for a while.

Uranus/Neptune
- ~ Mysticism, astrology and the desire to learn characterise this aspect.
- ~ You could become caught up in almost anything that is otherworldly.
- ~ Guard against drink or drugs.

Uranus/Pluto
- ~ Major changes that are happening out in the world may affect your lifestyle in a major way.
- ~ You could change direction radically and leave everything behind in order to start again.
- ~ Powerful feelings come to the surface.

Uranus/Nodes
- ~ You could develop an interest in astrology or spiritual matters.
- ~ Friends or groups will influence your life in some way.
- ~ Karmic benefits.
- ~ You may take up politics or something else that involves the public.

Uranus/Ascendant
- ~ A complete change of lifestyle is probable.
- ~ You may break out of your mould and leave some important part of your life behind.
- ~ Groups of people and friends will have an important bearing on your life.
- ~ You may become interested in astrology or something similar.

Uranus/Midheaven
- ~ A change of job or a complete change of direction is likely.
- ~ You may become attracted to electronics, astrology, computers or other modern techniques.
- ~ You may take up humanitarian work.

Neptune/Neptune
- ~ This is a good time for creative projects or for art, photography, film or anything else that creates an illusion.
- ~ You may fall in love and you won't be able to see straight as a result.
- ~ You may come to terms with something that went wrong in your past.
- ~ Something could be revealed.

Neptune/Pluto
- ~ Some kind of major change is affecting your life, and this could be a political or world situation.
- ~ You may fall in love, take up an artistic career or change your life entirely in some way.

Neptune/Nodes
- ~ You may decide to move your home close to the sea or a source of water.
- ~ Love could affect your lifestyle, your job and your family situation.
- ~ You may do something for others that creates karmic benefit.

Neptune/Ascendant
- ~ An increase in your spirituality or creativity.
- ~ You may fall in love or you may be a prey to illusions.
- ~ Film, photography or art may become important.
- ~ You may become psychic.

20: The Slower Moving Planets

Neptune/Midheaven
- A career in an artistic field is likely.
- You may become interested in cosmetics, hairdressing, film, photography or art.
- You may fall in love with someone whom you meet through work.
- You may become psychic.

Pluto/Pluto
- You may appear to change your life suddenly but the chances are that this change has been on the cards for years.

Pluto/Nodes
- A change of address and a change of family circumstances are possible.
- You may seek to influence events now or you may be influenced by the prevailing political situation.
- Karmic benefits might be on the way.

Pluto/Ascendant
- A change of direction is likely.
- You may feel paralysed and unable to make changes but subtle alterations are going on somewhere deep down inside you.
- You could take an interest in big business or in shared or joint ventures.

Pluto/Midheaven
- A terrific time for influencing the world that you live in.
- Political or other situations may give you opportunities for advancement.
- You will deal with taxes, corporate matters and anything that arises through joint financial matters.

Chiron
- Aspects to or by Chiron affect health and sometimes one's state of mind. On a positive note, they can also relate to education, sports, sporting achievements and even an interest in music. Check out the other planets or the angles that are involved in the progression or transit to see which body part is likely to be affected, or whatever else might turn up at this time.

Nodes, Asc, MC, Dsc, IC

It is hard to quantify the changes that movements of the angles bring, but you can pick up clues by looking at the natal planets that are affected.

- ~ The nodes can be associated with premises, emotions, family, parents and karma. I recently read a book on Thai astrology, and, while the systems were totally incomprehensible, the Thai take on the planets was interesting, especially where the Moon's nodes are concerned. The Thais seem to reverse our ideas and those of the Hindu astrologers, because they consider the south node to be a very good point on a horoscope. It represents honesty, decency, an upright nature, a good worker, common sense and all kinds of good things. However, they dislike the north node intensely, and consider it to be a very bad influence indeed, as they link it to obsession, addiction, a lack of backbone or moral fibre, and altogether a bad thing. I have checked out their ideas on several charts with some very interesting results, so I suggest that you try this for yourself.
- ~ The Asc concerns the self.
- ~ The MC denotes aims, ambitions and the future. In some cases, it concerns the father.
- ~ The Dsc indicates other people.
- ~ The IC harks back to the past, to the background to a situation, to the family, the mother and the home.

Conclusion

This book cannot contain all that is possible where predictive astrology is concerned, so use it as a good starting point and keep it handy as a reference book for those times that you need to refer back to an idea. Do read anything and everything that you can find on predictive astrology, and do as many charts for friends and relatives as you can while you are learning.

I hope you enjoy this book, and I wish you the very best of luck.
Sasha Fenton

~~~~~~~~~~~~~~~~~~

Zambezi Publishing Ltd

If you enjoyed this book, please have a look at our wide range of mind, body & spirit books; more of our titles are being reworked as eBooks as well.

Visit our website for a full listing - www.zampub.com or look through any major Internet bookshop; UK sites hold all our titles, USA sites will have just the USA editions.

Also, visit Sasha Fenton's author page on Amazon.co.uk and Amazon.com for an extensive list of her books.

Index

90-Degree Arc 15

A
Ages of Change 54
air 64
Amor 24
Aquarius 61
Arabic Parts 24
Arc, Ninety-Degree 57
arcs, Martian 16
Arcs, Martian 58
Arcs, Venusian 16
Aries 59
Asc 27, 28, 118
Asc, solar return 46
ascendant 7, 27
Aspects 35
aspects in Susan's chart 43
Aspects, Contra-Parallel 39
aspects, major 37
aspects, natal 35
aspects, Parallel 39
aspects, transiting 35
Asteroids 24
Astrologer's Calendar 6
Astrology, Electional 17, 58
Astrology, Horary 17, 58
Astrology, Mundane 17, 58

B
beneficial 35

Bi-quintile 39
birth time 33
births, daytime 25
births, night time 25
Boyle, Susan 39
Britain's Got Talent 39
Bruno 55

C

Cancer 60, 77
Capricorn 61
cardinal 63, 64
centaur 24
Ceres 24
challenging 35
charts, Electional 35
Chiron 24, 29, 31, 60, 117
conjunction 37
Conjunction 37
conjunction, triple 36
contra-parallels 39
Culpeper, Nicholas 16
Cycles, Planetary 49

D

decans 63
Decans 65
Decumbitures 16, 58
Dee, Jonathan 5, 10
descendant 27
Diana 24
directions, solar arc 12
Directions, Solar Arc 57
Directions, Solar Return 15
Divisions, Ancient 66
Dsc 27, 118
Dwaads 13

E

earth 64
Earth 45, 50
eccentric orbits 53
eclipse 32
eclipse, lunar 47
eclipse, solar 47
Eclipses 47
ecliptic 39
Ecliptic 24
Elements 64
Ephemeris 19
Eros 24
exalted 63

F

feminine 63
fire 64
fixed 26, 64
Fred 19

G

Gemini 59
Genders 63

H

Half Cycle 55
half-return, Uranus 49
half-returns, Jupiter 51
Hidalgo 24
horary 35
House Rulers 17
House, Eighth 60
House, Eleventh 61
House, Fifth 60
House, First 59
House, Fourth 60
House, Ninth 61

House, Second 59
House, Seventh 60
House, Sixth 60
House, Tenth 61
House, Third 59
House, Twelfth 61
Houses 8
Huber Jupiter Cycle 55
Huber, Louise 55
Huberism 55
humours 16

I
IC 27, 118
Icarus 24
Inconjunct 38

J
Jove 51
Juno 24
Jupiter 29, 31, 51, 61
Jupiter/Ascendant 114
Jupiter/Jupiter 113
Jupiter/Midheaven 114
Jupiter/Neptune 113
Jupiter/Pluto 113
Jupiter/Saturn 113
Jupiter/the Nodes 114
Jupiter/Uranus 113

K
karmic points 24
Kethu 24
Koch 77
Kuala Lumpur 32

L
Leo 60

Libra 60
Lilith 24
Lilly, William 16
Lunar month 13

M

malefic 10
Mars 29, 31, 50, 59, 60
Mars/Ascendant 112
Mars/Chiron 111
Mars/Jupiter 109
Mars/Mars 109
Mars/Midheaven 112
Mars/Neptune 110
Mars/Pluto 111
Mars/Saturn 110
Mars/the Nodes 111
Mars/Uranus 110
MC 27, 28, 46, 118
Mercury 29, 31, 50, 59, 60
Mercury/Ascendant 106
Mercury/Chiron 105
Mercury/Jupiter 102
Mercury/Mars 102
Mercury/Mercury 101
Mercury/Midheaven 106
Mercury/Neptune 104
Mercury/Pluto 104
Mercury/Saturn 103
Mercury/the Nodes 105
Mercury/Uranus 103
Mercury/Venus 101
midheaven 27
Midpoints 23
Milky Way 26
Moon 29, 31, 50, 60
Moon through Aquarius 83
Moon through Aries 78

Moon through Cancer 80
Moon through Capricorn 83
Moon through Gemini 79
Moon through Leo 80
Moon through Libra 81
Moon through Pisces 84
Moon through Sagittarius 82
Moon through Scorpio 82
Moon through Taurus 79
Moon through Virgo 81
Moon/Ascendant 99
Moon/Chiron 99
Moon/Jupiter 95
Moon/Mars 95
Moon/Mercury 93
Moon/Midheaven 100
Moon/Moon 93
Moon/Neptune 97
Moon/Pluto 98
Moon/Saturn 96
Moon/the Nodes 99
Moon/Uranus 96
Moon/Venus 94
Moons 24
Mount Olympus 51
mutable 64

N
nadir 27
Neptune 28, 30, 53, 61
Neptune/Ascendant 117
Neptune/Midheaven 117
Neptune/Neptune 116
Neptune/Nodes 116
Neptune/Pluto 116
nodes 118
Nodes of the Moon 24, 29, 31
Nodes, Asc, MC, Dsc, IC 118

North Node 24

O
opposition 37
Opposition 37
Orbs 35

P
Pallas Athena 24
Pandora 24
parallels 39
Part of Fortune 25, 37
Perpetual Noon Date 18, 58
Pisces 61
Placidus 77
planet, "breakout" 53
Planetoids 24
Pluto 28, 30, 53, 60
Pluto/Ascendant 117
Pluto/Midheaven 117
Pluto/Nodes 117
Pluto/Pluto 117
portents of evil 48
Precession 45
Prediction Magazine 5
Progressions 11, 23
progressions by hand 19
Progressions, Daily House 18, 58
progressions, day-for-a-year 11
Progressions, Day-for-a-Year 57
Progressions, Duodenary 57
progressions, solar arc 12, 45
progressions, tertiary 13
Psyche 24

Q
Qualities 64
Quintile 38

quintile, progressed 38

R
Rahu 24
Raphael's Ephemeris 2
Rectification 18
retrograde motion 29, 49
return, Jupiter 51
return, lunar 50
return, Saturn 49
returns, lunar 11, 35
Returns, Lunar 16, 46, 57
returns, solar 11
returns, Solar 45
Returns, Solar 15, 57
Romans 48

S
Sagittarius 61
Sappho 24
Saturn 29, 31, 51, 61
Saturn/Ascendant 115
Saturn/Midheaven 115
Saturn/Neptune 114
Saturn/Nodes 115
Saturn/Pluto 114
Saturn/Saturn 114
Saturn/Uranus 114
secondary directions 11
Semi-sextile 38
Semi-square 38
sensitive point 36
Sesquiquadrate 38
Sextile 38
Signs 8
signs, air 64
Signs, Air 66
signs, earth 64

INDEX

Signs, Earth 65
signs, fire 64
Signs, Fire 65
signs, Masculine 63
signs, water 64
Signs, Water 66
software 9
Solar Arc MC progressions 12
Solar Fire 12
Solar system 50
South Node 24
square 37
Square 38
stellium, natal 36
Sun 29, 31, 50, 60, 69
Sun through Aquarius 74
Sun through Aries 70
Sun through Cancer 71
Sun through Capricorn 74
Sun through Gemini 71
Sun through Leo 71
Sun through Libra 72
Sun through Pisces 75
Sun through Sagittarius 73
Sun through Scorpio 73
Sun through Taurus 70
Sun through Virgo 72
Sun/Ascendant 92
Sun/Chiron 91
Sun/Jupiter 88
Sun/Mars 87
Sun/Mercury 86
Sun/Midheaven 92
Sun/Moon 85
Sun/Neptune 90
Sun/Pluto 91
Sun/Saturn 88
Sun/Sun 85

Sun/the Nodes 92
Sun/Uranus 89
Sun/Venus 86

T
Taurus 59
Toro 24
transit, lunar 9
transit, retrograde 10
transits 23
Transits 9, 30, 57
trine 37
Trine 37
twins 3

U
Urania 24
Uranus 28, 30, 53, 61
Uranus half 53
Uranus squares 53
Uranus/Ascendant 116
Uranus/Midheaven 116
Uranus/Neptune 115
Uranus/Nodes 116
Uranus/Pluto 115
Uranus/Uranus 115

V
Venus 29, 31, 50, 59, 60
Venus/Ascendant 109
Venus/Chiron 108
Venus/Jupiter 107
Venus/Mars 106
Venus/Midheaven 109
Venus/Neptune 108
Venus/Pluto 108
Venus/Saturn 107
Venus/the Nodes 108

Venus/Uranus 107
Venus/Venus 106
Vertex 25, 37
Vesta 24
Virgo 60

W
Warren-Davis, Dylan 16
water 64

Y
yod 38

Z
zodiac 63
Zodiac List 6

Zambezi Publishing Ltd

We hope you have enjoyed reading this book. The Zambezi range of books includes titles by top level, internationally acknowledged authors on fresh, thought-provoking viewpoints in your favourite subjects. A common thread with all our books is the easy accessibility of content; we have no sleep-inducing tomes, just down-to-earth, easily digestible, credible books.

~~~~~

Please visit our website (www.zampub.com) to browse our full range of Lifestyle and Mind, Body & Spirit titles, and to discover what might spark your interest next...

Please note:-

Some of our books are already available as eBooks, including the Kindle format, and we intend to digitise many more. Visit our website from time to time for more details, or check Amazon.co.uk, Amazon.com and other major Internet bookshops as well.

Our books are available from good bookshops throughout the UK, but nowadays, no bookshop can hope to carry in stock more than a fraction of the books published each year (over 200,000 new titles were published in the UK last year!). However, most UK bookshops can order and supply our titles swiftly, in no more than a few days (within the UK).

You can also find all our books on amazon.co.uk, other UK internet bookshops, and many are also on amazon.com - sometimes under different titles and ISBNs. Look for the author's name.

Our website (www.zampub.com) also carries and sells our whole range, direct to you. If you prefer not to use the Internet for book purchases, you are welcome to contact us direct (our address is at the front of this book, and on our website) for pricing and payment methods.

www.ingramcontent.com/pod-product-compliance
Lightning Source LLC
LaVergne TN
LVHW051608070426
835507LV00021B/2830